Project Manager: Carol Cuellar
Book Art Layout: Joe Klucar
Album Art: © 2003 Warner Music Group
Album Art Direction: Jeri Heiden for SMOG Design, Inc. and Hugh Brown
Design: Ryan Corey & Jeri Heiden for SMOG Design, Inc.
Cover Artwork and Lettering: Boyd Elder.com
Photos: Henry Diltz, Jim Shea, John Halpern and James R. Minchin III

CONTENTS

From left: Randy Meisner, Glenn Frey, Bernie Leadon, and Don Henley

Photo: Henry Diltz

CONVERSATIONS WITH

DON HENLEY AND GLENN FREY

by Cameron Crowe • August 2003

TAKE IT EASY

GLENN: Jackson Browne, J.D. Souther, and I all lived at 1020 Laguna in Echo Park. J.D. and I shared a $60-a-month, one-room apartment—a couch and kind of a bed with a curtain in front of it. Right underneath us in an even smaller studio apartment was Jackson. He had his piano and guitars down there. I didn't really know how to sit down and work on a song until I heard him playing underneath us in the basement. He would work on "Jamaica Say You Will," and he had the first verse and chorus. Then he would sing the second verse—sing it five or six times—and then silence. Twenty seconds later, he would start again and sing the second verse this time, and, if he liked it, he'd sing it over and over again. I had never really witnessed that sort of focus—someone being that fastidious—and it gave me a different idea about how to write songs; that maybe it wasn't all just going to be a flood of inspiration. That's when I first heard "Take It Easy."

Photos: Henry Diltz

DON: We gave Glenn a nickname, The Lone Arranger. He had a vision about how our voices could blend and how to arrange the vocals and, in many cases, the tracks. He also had a knack for remembering and choosing good songs. Jackson had shelved "Take It Easy" because he couldn't complete it, but it was Glenn who remembered the song from some time earlier and asked Jackson about it one day.

GLENN: I told him that I really liked it. "What was that, man? What a cool tune that is." He started playing it for me and said, "Yeah, but I don't know—I'm stuck." So he played the second unfinished verse and I said, "It's a girl, my lord, in a flatbed Ford, slowin' down to take a look at me." That was my contribution to "Take It Easy," really, just finishing the second verse. Jackson was so thrilled. He said, "Okay! We cowrote this." But it's certainly more of him. Sometimes, you know, it's the package without the ribbon. He already had the lines about Winslow, Arizona. He'd had car trouble and broken down there on one of his trips to Sedona. He spent a long day in Winslow. . . . I don't know that we could have ever had a better opening song on our first album. Just those opening chords felt like an announcement, "And now . . . the Eagles."

WITCHY WOMAN

DON: Bernie and I just sort of stumbled upon "Witchy Woman." I was living in an old house in the Hollywood Hills on the corner of Camrose and Tower, near the Hollywood Bowl. Bernie was living way out in Topanga Canyon, but he came over one day and started playing this strange, minor-key riff that sounded sort of like a Hollywood movie version of Indian music—you know, the kind of stuff they play when the Indians ride up on the ridge while the wagon train passes below. It had a haunting quality, and I thought it was interesting, so we put a rough version of it down on a cassette tape. Shortly after that, I came down with the flu. I had a very high fever and became semi-delirious at times—and that's when I wrote most of the lyrics. Every time the fever

Photo: Henry Diltz

subsided, I would continue to read a new book I'd gotten on the life of Zelda Fitzgerald, and I think that figured into the mix somehow—along with amorphous images of girls I had met at the Whisky and the Troubadour. An important song for me, because it marked the beginning of my professional songwriting career. It went to #9 in the charts.

PEACEFUL EASY FEELING

GLENN: Well, it reminded me so much of Poco. Compared to the original recording, it's evolved through live performances to where it's a bit of a different animal now. Back then, Poco was the band that impressed me most. Their vocals were pristine and perfect. They were the band I wanted to model us after. We loved all the singing bands—The Byrds and The Beach Boys—but to be honest, right then I had my eye on Poco . . . and I wanted to go beyond them too. Ironically, we'd have two bass players over the years, both from Poco. "Peaceful Easy Feeling" had a happy, country-rock quality but a bittersweet irony about it that I thought was really great. I still love that song. Love singing it.

DESPERADO

DON: "Desperado" was a song fragment that I'd had since the late '60s. Maybe '68, I started that song. It wasn't even called "Desperado." It was called something else, but it was the same melody, same chords. I think it had something to do with astrology [chuckles]. Whatever the title was back then, it was horrible [laughs]. Jackson Browne suggested a Western theme—something to do with playing cards, I think—which is sort of where we were headed anyway. When we returned from England, after making our first album, I was living in a little house, way up in Laurel Canyon. I think Roger McGuinn had lived there previously. It was one of those houses on stilts, and when the winds were high, the house would rock gently. It was sort of unsettling, but I got used to it after a while.

Anyway, Glenn came over to write one day, and I showed him this unfinished tune that I had been holding for so many years. I said, "When I play it and sing it, I think of Ray Charles—Ray Charles and Stephen Foster. It's really a Southern gothic thing, but we can easily make it more Western." Glenn leapt right on it—filled in the blanks and brought structure. And that was the beginning of our songwriting partnership . . . that's when we became a team.

GLENN: It was only a day or two after we had been back from England with our first album. Don sat down at the piano and showed me this song he was working on, and it was the intro to "Desperado." Originally, it was written for a friend of his whose name was Leo. And so the song started out "Leo, my God, why don't you come to your senses. You've been out ridin' fences for so long now." We'd all been to the Troubadour to see Tim Hardin, and later the four of us, Jackson, J.D. Souther, Don, and myself went to somebody's house . . . it wasn't mine. I don't know if it was J.D.'s, but we went somewhere and started jamming. That's when the idea came together about us doing an album of all the angst-meisters [laughs]. It was going to be all of the antiheroes. James Dean was going to be one song, and the Doolin-Dalton gang was going to be another. The idea became "Desperado," and Don's Stephen Foster song acquired a new first line—"Desperado . . . why don't you come to your senses?" That same week we wrote "Desperado" and "Tequila Sunrise." I think I brought him ideas and a lot of opinions; he brought me poetry—we were a good team.

TEQUILA SUNRISE

DON: I believe that was a Glenn title. I think he was ambivalent about it because he thought that it was a bit too obvious or too much of a cliché because of the drink that was so popular then. I said "No—look at it from a different point of view. You've been drinking straight tequila all night, and the sun is coming up!" It turned out to be a really great song. The changes that Glenn came up with for the bridge are very smart. That's one song I don't get tired of. "Take another shot of courage" refers to tequila—because we used to call it "instant courage." We very much wanted to talk to the ladies, but we often didn't have the nerve, so we'd drink a couple of shots and suddenly it was, "Howdy, ma'am."

GLENN: I love the song. I think the goal of any songwriter is to make a song appear seamless, to never show the struggle. Nothing should sound forced. "Tequila Sunrise" was written fairly quickly, and I don't think there's a single chord out of place.

DOOLIN-DALTON

DON: Jackson, J.D., and Glenn had all started on this idea before I even got to California. Apparently, it began with a book on gunfighters that somebody—Ned Doheny, I believe—had given them when they were living in Echo Park. As we were writing the song "Desperado" I guess we had that in mind, and so the theme turned decidedly Western. You know, mythical, majestic images of the great American Southwest . . . or as Donald Fagen later called it, "cowboy dream crap" [laughs]. Anyway, it was a time of great openness and camaraderie. There was a willingness to collaborate and there was a lot of mutual support and encouragement, which I thought was wonderful. In that atmosphere I began to come into my own as a songwriter. It was great having the opportunity to write with all those guys, because they were so damned opinionated. "This is crap. That's brilliant. That's crap." I loved it. None of us had really accomplished much up to that point, but there were big plans and strong opinions flying around everywhere.

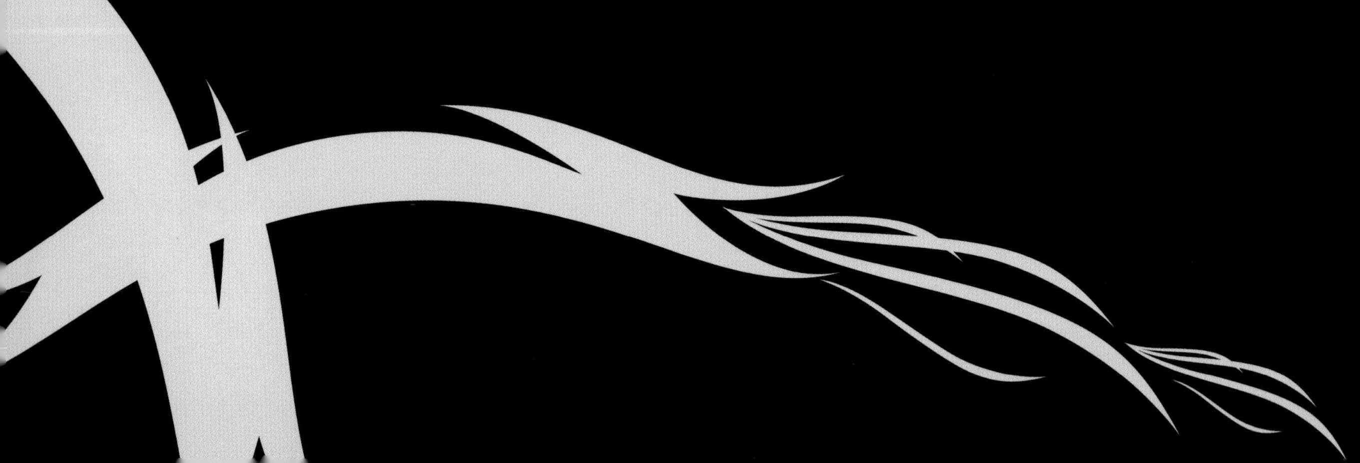

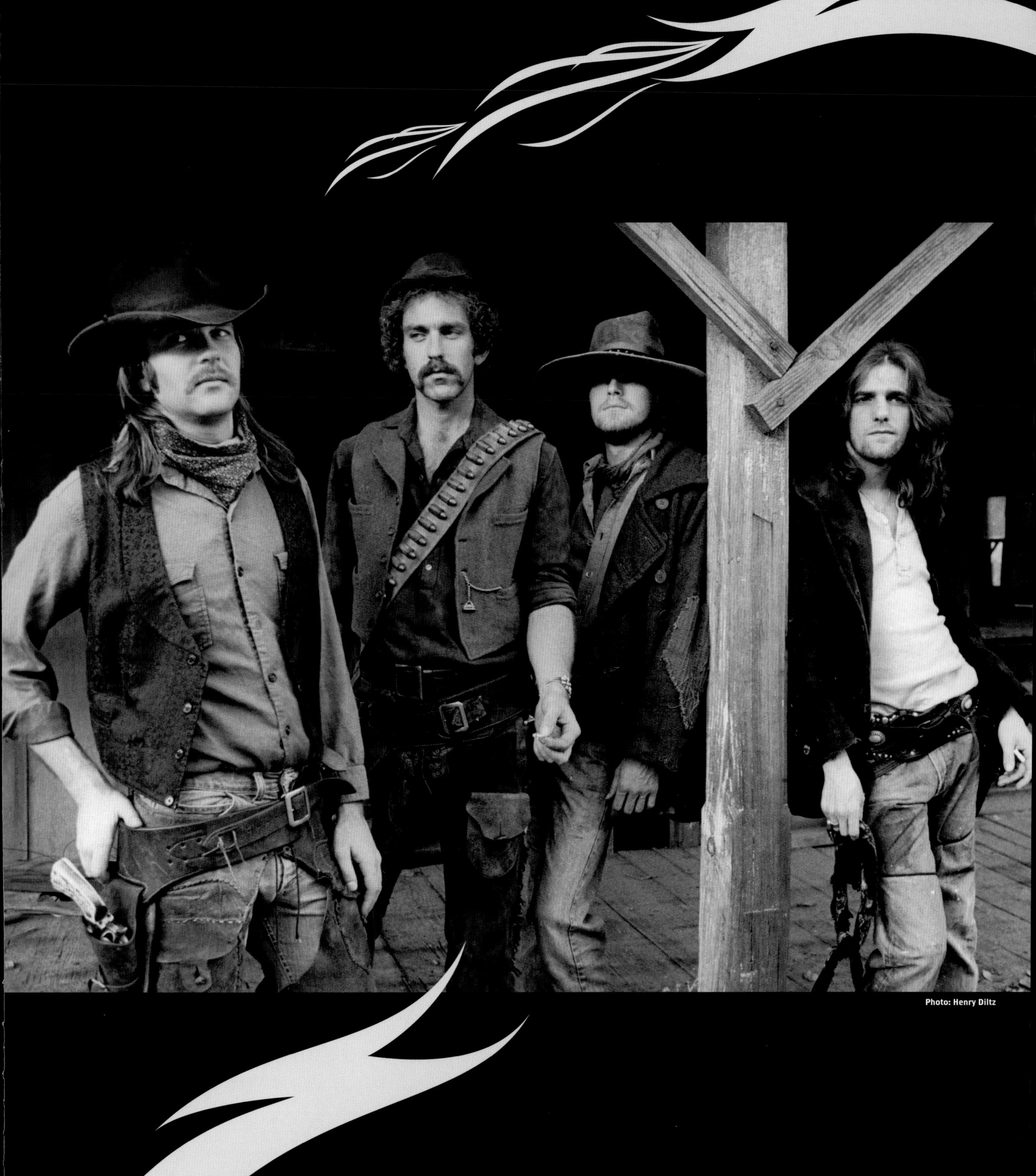

Photo: Henry Diltz

Photo: Henry Diltz

ALREADY GONE

GLENN: I got a tape of the song from Jack Tempchin in my mailbox at 1740 La Fontaine Ct., the house in Coldwater Canyon where I lived for 16 years. James Cagney's brother, Ed, had once owned the house, and it still holds a lot of memories for me. James Cagney, in his later years, sometimes used the house as a hideaway and went there to play the piano and relax. In earlier years, the Cagneys held great parties in that bungalow. A lot of music happened there.

"Already Gone," though, arrived in the mail. Jack was a songwriter we liked who was from San Diego, and he'd already written "Peaceful Easy Feeling." "Already Gone" was one of the first songs we'd later do when we switched producers and started recording in Los Angeles. I had a very strained relationship with Glyn Johns. I think he got along better with all the other guys in the band. He was so intimidating, I was always afraid to be forthright and tell him what I thought. He was a taskmaster, and that was probably good for a young band, but the great thing for me about this song and record is that I left England behind and had a much more positive energy in the recording studio. The "all right, nighty-night" at the end of the song was sort of typical of the spontaneous feeling we wanted on our records. It was at this time that we changed producers and started working with Bill Szymczyk. I was much more comfortable in the studio with Bill, and he was more than willing to let everyone stretch a bit. "Already Gone"—that's me being happier; that's me being free.

THE BEST OF MY LOVE

DON: A lot of the lyrics were actually written in Dan Tana's at a booth we liked to sit in, on the front side of the bar area. J.D. Souther wrote the bridge and it was perfect. That was the period when there were all these great-looking girls who didn't really want to have anything to do with us. We were just scruffy new kids who had no calling card. We could be cocky at times—which was really just a front—but we weren't very sophisticated or confident. We were typical, frustrated, young men. We wanted the girls to like us, but we had all the immature emotions that young men have—jealousy, envy, frustration, lust, insecurity, and the lot. At the same time, however, we were also becoming quite adept at brushing off girls who showed any interest in us. "If you want to be with me, I can't possibly give you the time of day. I want that girl over there who couldn't care less if I live or die." Hence the line in "Desperado": "You only want the ones that you can't get." We knew ourselves even then. Even in our immaturity we had some insight into our flawed little characters [rueful laughter]. Shaw was right—"Youth is wasted on the young."

GLENN: I was playing acoustic guitar one afternoon in Laurel Canyon, and I was trying to figure out a tuning that Joni Mitchell had shown me a couple of days earlier. I got lost and ended up with the guitar tuning for what would later turn out to be "The Best Of My Love."

JAMES DEAN

GLENN: Again, all from that same night when we'd gone to see Tim Hardin. As *Desperado* became a concept album with an Old West theme, "James Dean" got shelved. When it came time to do *On The Border*, we got "James Dean" right off the shelf and said, "Let's finish this." I always thought the best line in "James Dean" was "I know my life would look alright if I could see it on the silver screen." You just don't get to do that.

DON: I sat there and listened to the guys talk about James Dean. They had evidently studied him and knew much more about him than I did. I had seen most of Dean's movies, but I somehow missed the whole icon thing. The mythology never quite reached my part of East Texas, but I pitched in and ended up with a writing credit—although the song was mostly Jackson's, I think.

OL' 55

GLENN: David Geffen played me a tape of Tom Waits in his office. "Ol' 55" was the first song on a demo that had maybe three songs on it. I loved the song, got Tom Waits' version, and took it to the band. I played it for Don and said, "I think we should do this. We can split the vocals, it could be really cool, and we could do *ooooh*s in this section here." I really liked the song. Still do. It's such a car thing. Your first car is like your first apartment. You had a mobile studio apartment! "Ol' 55" was so Southern California, and yet there was some Detroit in it as well. It was that car thing, and I loved the idea of driving home at sunrise, thinking about what had happened the night before.

MIDNIGHT FLYER

DON: I was happy to do something in that vein, because I was a big bluegrass fan. The Dillards, in particular, had an enormous impact on me. Along with Doug Dillard and Herb Pedersen, Bernie Leadon was one of the top banjo players in the country, so I was proud to do a bluegrass tune—thought it lent a certain amount of authenticity and credibility to our band. It showed versatility.

Even now the Eagles are thought of as a country-rock band. The music industry and the media saddled us with that label at the very beginning, and, no matter how diverse our musical palate, it has been impossible to shake that stereotype. At the end of the day, we're an American band. We're a musical mutt with influences from every genre of American popular music. It's all in there, and it's fairly obvious.

From left: Glenn Frey, Don Felder, Randy Meisner (in car), Bernie Leadon, and Don Henley

Photo: Henry Diltz

ON THE BORDER

DON: This track turned out to be completely different from what I had envisioned. There was a clash of styles and influences in that song, and I'm not sure it ever became what it could have been, musically. As for the lyrics, there was a lot going on in the country at that time regarding the impeachment of Richard Nixon. The whole Watergate debacle was coming to a head. Interestingly, not unlike now, there were a lot of people concerned about the government overstepping its bounds with regard to issues of privacy. It's much like the Ashcroft world we're looking at today. So that's what the verses ended up being about. It's an odd song. I like Glenn's cool little R&B guitar part in the tag, though, and at the very end there's something almost inaudible. Someone—it had to be Glenn or me—says, "Say goodnight, Dick," which was a phrase made famous on The Smothers Brothers' show when Tommy says, "Say goodnight, Dick." We were addressing Nixon, because at that time it was pretty clear that he was on his way out, so that was our little kiss-off to Tricky Dick.

LYIN' EYES

DON: "Lyin' Eyes" is one of the songs written when Glenn and I were roommates in a house we rented up in Trousdale. It was built in 1942 by the actress Dorothy Lamour. Glenn and I lived at opposite ends of the house and we actually converted a music room to a full-on recording studio. The house was located at the highest point on the hill and we had a 360-degree panorama. In the daytime, we could see snowcapped peaks to the east and the blue Pacific to the west. At night, the twinkling lights of the city below were breathtaking. The place had a couple of nicknames—"The House With The Million Dollar View" and "The Eagles' Nest," of course. We had some great times up there. As for "Lyin' Eyes," Glenn's pretty much responsible for that track and for the title, the choruses. I helped out with the verses and perhaps with the melody. It's really Glenn's baby.

GLENN: The house was up on Briarcrest Lane. That's where we wrote "One Of These Nights," "Lyin' Eyes," "Take It To The Limit," "After The Thrill Is Gone," and a couple of other tunes for the *One Of These Nights* album. But "Lyin' Eyes"—the story had always been there. I don't want to say it wrote itself, but once we started working on it, there were no sticking points. Lyrics just kept coming out, and that's not always the way songs get written. I think songwriting is a lot like pushing a boulder up a hill. I'd love to get the legal pad for "Lyin' Eyes" again, because I think there were verses we didn't use.

ONE OF THESE NIGHTS

DON: We'd started to explore our love of rhythm & blues and the Gamble & Huff records that came out of Philadelphia. We were also huge fans of Al Green. Glenn was the catalyst for this song. I think he sat down with a guitar and started playing that rhythm part [sings it]. It was another song from the "Lyin' Eyes" house. We like to call it our "satanic country-rock period" [laughs]. Because it was a dark time, both politically and musically, in America. There was turmoil in Washington and disco music was starting to take off. We thought, "Well, how can we write something with that flavor, with that kind of beat, and still have the dangerous guitars?" We wanted to capture the spirit of the times. So, perched up there on top of that hill, almost all night, every night, we had a big, phantasmagorical scene which included songwriting and, uh—research. Lots of research.

The song is a great showcase for high harmony. Meisner hit some notes that only dogs could hear. We also started getting into harmony parts on guitars that simulated horn riffs. It was a cool record.

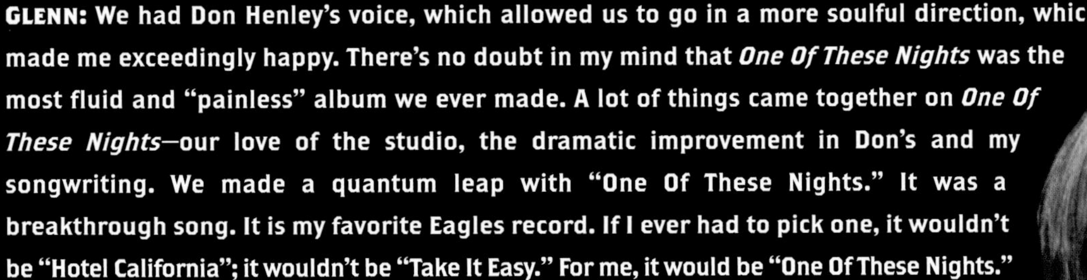

GLENN: We had Don Henley's voice, which allowed us to go in a more soulful direction, which made me exceedingly happy. There's no doubt in my mind that *One Of These Nights* was the most fluid and "painless" album we ever made. A lot of things came together on *One Of These Nights*—our love of the studio, the dramatic improvement in Don's and my songwriting. We made a quantum leap with "One Of These Nights." It was a breakthrough song. It is my favorite Eagles record. If I ever had to pick one, it wouldn't be "Hotel California"; it wouldn't be "Take It Easy." For me, it would be "One Of These Nights."

Photo: Henry Diltz

TAKE IT TO THE LIMIT

GLENN: I just remember being very happy for Randy. We had tried, unsuccessfully, to get a piece of material for him—or from him—that might be a hit single, or turn into one. I don't think we ever consciously tried to make hit singles. We finally succeeded with "Take It To The Limit." That's the first Eagles single to sell a million copies. It was our first gold single, maybe our only gold single. People always tended to buy our albums instead. We still had hit records, but they wouldn't sell through as 45s much. We had a lot of #1s, but I know that "Take It To The Limit" was our first gold single. And when Randy would sing it in Japan—it was *mass hysteria* [laughs].

AFTER THE THRILL IS GONE

DON: "After The Thrill Is Gone" is something of an overlooked song that I think is very good. It's me and Glenn, working together. He did the verses with a little help from me. I did the bridge. As exciting as the whole Eagles thing was at times, some of the luster was beginning to wear off. We were combining our personal and professional lives in song.

GLENN: It's a sleeper. That record is a lot of self-examination, hopefully not too much. There was a lot of double-meaning and a lot of irony. "Any kind of love without passion/Well, that ain't no kind of lovin' at all . . . "—pure Henley.

HOTEL CALIFORNIA

GLENN: The song began as a demo tape, an instrumental by Don Felder. He'd been submitting tapes and song ideas to us since he'd joined the band, always instrumentals, since he didn't sing. But this particular demo, unlike many of the others, had room for singing. It immediately got our attention. The first working title, the name we gave it, was "Mexican Reggae."

For us, "Hotel California" was definitely thinking and writing outside the box. We had never written any song like it before. Similar to "Desperado," we did not start out to make any sort of concept or theme album. But when we wrote "Life In The Fast Lane" and started working on "Hotel California" and "New Kid In Town" with J.D., we knew we were heading down a long and twisted corridor and just stayed with it. Songs from the dark side—the Eagles take a look at the seamy underbelly of L.A.—the flip side of fame and failure, love and money.

"They stab it with their steely knives, but they just can't kill the beast" was a little Post-It back to Steely Dan. Apparently, Walter Becker's girlfriend loved the Eagles, and she played them all the time. I think it drove him nuts. So, the story goes that they were having a fight one day, and that was the genesis of the line, "turn up the Eagles, the neighbors are listening" in "Everything You Did," from Steely Dan's *The Royal Scam* album. During the writing of "Hotel California," we decided to volley. We just wanted to allude to Steely Dan rather than mentioning them outright, so "Dan" got changed to "knives," which is still, you know, a penile metaphor. Stabbing, thrusting, etc.

Almost everybody in my business can write music, play guitar, play piano, create chord progressions, etc., but it's only when you add lyrics and melody and voices to these things that they take on an identity and become something beyond the sum of the individual parts. I remember that Henley and I were listening to the "Hotel California" demo tape together on an airplane, and we were talking about what we would write and how we wanted to be more cinematic. We wanted this song to open like an episode of *The Twilight Zone*—just one shot after another.

I remember De Niro in *The Last Tycoon*. He's got this scene, and he's talking to some other people in his office. He speaks to them: "The door opens . . . the camera is on a person's feet . . . he walks across the room . . . we pan up to the table . . . he picks up a pack of matches that says 'The Such-And-Such Club' on it . . . strikes a match and lights a cigarette . . . puts it out . . . goes over to the window . . . opens the shade . . . looks out . . . the moon is there . . . what does it mean? Nothing. It's just the movies." "Hotel California" is like that. We take this guy and make him like a character in *The Magus*, where every time he walks through a door there's a new version of reality. We wanted to write a song just like it was a movie. This guy is driving across the desert. He's tired. He's smokin'. Comes up over a hill, sees some lights, pulls in. First thing he sees is a really strange guy at the front door, welcoming him: "Come on in." Walks in, and then it becomes Fellini-esque—strange women, effeminate men, shadowy corridors, disembodied voices, debauchery, illusion. . . . Weirdness. So we thought, "Let's really take some chances. Let's try to write in a way that we've never written before." Steely Dan inspired us because of their lyrical bravery and willingness to go "out there." So, for us, "Hotel California" was about thinking and writing outside the box.

DON: We were enamored with hotels. Hotels were a big part of our lives. The Beverly Hills Hotel had become something of a focal point—literally and symbolically. I've always been interested in architecture and the language of architecture, and, at that time, I was particularly keen on the mission style of early California. I thought there was a certain mystery and romance about it. Then, there are all the great movies and plays in which hotels figure prominently, not only as a structure, but as a dramatic device. Films such as *Grand Hotel*, *The Night Porter*, and even *Psycho*—motels count too. There are plays like Neil Simon's *Plaza Suite* and *California Suite*, which Glenn and I went to see while writing the song. We saw it as homework or research. We were looking for things that would stimulate us and give us ideas. Sometimes it was just driving around. We would still take trips out to the desert. At one point, Glenn and I rented a little red house up in Idlewild—way up in the San Bernardino Mountains. We'd drive out there sometimes just to clear our heads, sleep on the floor in sleeping bags. We didn't have any furniture. We were just on the quest.

LIFE IN THE FAST LANE

GLENN: This began with a Joe Walsh riff—he had that signature guitar part. I had the title. The true story is: I was riding in a car with a drug dealer—a guy we used to call "The Count," because his count was never very good [laughs]. We were driving out to an Eagles poker game. I was in the passenger seat. He moved over to the left lane and started driving 75-80 miles per hour. I said, "Hey, man, slow down." He goes, "Hey, man, it's life in the fast lane." And I thought, "Oh, my God, what a title." I didn't write it down. I didn't have to.

Joe started playing a riff at rehearsal one day, and I said, "That's 'Life In The Fast Lane.'" So we started writing a song about the couple that had everything and did everything—and lost the meaning of everything. Lifestyles of the rich and miserable. I think the best line is "We've been up and down this highway, haven't seen a God-damn thing." That pretty much summarized the journey these people were on—rich as hell, gettin' high, got everything they want, and yet they're living in a spiritual ghetto. That's good news to the common man. Rich folks who are absolutely miserable—and most of them are. I really like this record. Plus it made a statement: Joe Walsh was officially in the band.

WASTED TIME

GLENN: It's a Philly-soul torch song. I loved all the records coming out of Philadelphia at that time. I sent for some sheet music so I could learn some of those songs, and I started creating my own musical ideas with that Philly influence. Don was our Teddy Pendergrass. He could stand out there all alone and just wail. We did a big Philly-type production with strings—definitely not country rock. You're not going to find that track on a Crosby, Stills & Nash record or a Beach Boys record. Don's singing abilities stretched so many of our boundaries. He could sing the phone book. It didn't matter. We had Golden Throat [laughs appreciatively]. Jim Ed Norman, Don's old college buddy and former bandmate—and now President of Warner/Reprise Records/Nashville—wrote all of our string charts. He was right there with us in terms of wanting to do something like Thom Bell. It was definitely us loving Thom Bell.

GLENN: That's an Eagles track with no overdubs. It's five pieces, live. For a band that did a lot of overdubbing and a lot of editing, it was a neat thing to do. We just said, "Look, let's just cut this thing live and this will be it. It'll be what it is."

Photo: Jim Shea

Photo: Henry Diltz

THE LAST RESORT

GLENN: "The Last Resort" was the final piece of the *Hotel California* puzzle. We started the song early in the record, and Don finished seven months later. I called it Henley's opus. I helped describe what the song was going to be about and assisted with the arrangement, but it was Don's lyric and basic chord progression.

One of the primary themes of the song was that we keep creating what we've been running away from—violence, chaos, destruction. We migrated to the East Coast, killed a bunch of Indians, and just completely screwed that place up. Then we just kept moving west: "Move those teepees, we got some train tracks coming through here. Get outta the way, boy!" There were some very personal references in the song, including a girl from Providence, Rhode Island, who Don had dated for some time. She had taken an inheritance from her grandfather and moved to Aspen, Colorado, in search of a new life. Look where Aspen is now. How prophetic is "The Last Resort" 28 years after it was written? Aspen is a town where the billionaires have driven out the millionaires. It was once a great place. Look at Lahaina; look at Maui. It's so commercial. It's everything Hawaii was not supposed to be. Whether we're carrying the cross or carrying the gasoline can, we seem to have a penchant for wrecking beautiful places.

DON: The final burst on this one happened in Benedict Canyon at a house I was living in with Irving [Azoff, the band's longtime manager and friend]. I was thinking of all the literary themes based on nature that I had studied back in school—the awesome beauty and spirituality inherent in the natural world and the unrelenting destruction of it, wrought by this thing that we call

Some years earlier we had done a couple of benefit concerts with Neil Young for the Chumash Tribe, Native American people who are indigenous to California. We became friends with an elder in the tribe named Samu, and, eventually, we were invited to attend some tribal rituals and drum ceremonies. Samu was on a mission to raise funds for an education program which would teach the young people in the tribe about their language and their culture. The old man feared, rightly, that the white man's culture was stripping his people of their identity. They were losing the memory of their language, their ceremonies, their history. We were fortunate enough to be able to help.

Also, I'd been reading articles and doing research about the raping and pillaging of the West by mining, timber, oil and cattle interests. But I was interested in an even larger scope for the song, so I tried to go "Michener" with it. I remember going out to Malibu and standing on Zuma beach, looking out at the ocean. I remember thinking, "This is about as far west—with the exception of Alaska—as you can go on this continent. This is where Manifest Destiny ends—right here, in the middle of all these surfboards and volleyball nets and motor homes." And then I thought, "Nah, we've gone right on over and screwed up Hawaii too."

I still think, though, that the song was never fully realized, musically speaking. It's fairly pedestrian from a musical point of view. But lyrically it's not bad. Especially the last verse, which turns it from one thing into another and it becomes an allegorical statement about religion—the deception and destructiveness that is inherent in the mythology of most organized religion—the whole "dominion" thing. The song is a reaffirmation of the age-old idea that everything in the universe is connected and that there are consequences, downstream, for everything we do.

NEW KID IN TOWN

GLENN: We won a Grammy® for Best Vocal Arrangement for "New Kid In Town." I'm quite proud of that.

DON: J.D. Souther started the song. It's about the fleeting, fickle nature of love and romance. It's also about the fleeting nature of fame, especially in the music business. We were already chronicling our own demise [laughs]. We were basically saying, "Look, we know we're red hot right now, but we also know that somebody's going to come along and replace us—both in music and in love." We were always doing that double entendre thing, between the music business and personal relationships. But that song was J.D.'s baby—he was the father of that song.

PLEASE COME HOME FOR CHRISTMAS

DON: When I was growing up in East Texas, there were basically two radio stations that were interesting. There was KEEL in Shreveport, Louisiana, which I listened to in the daytime. Then there was the legendary WNOE in New Orleans, which I could pick up at night when the station boosted its signal. It broadcasted this wonderful, eclectic mix of music which was like nothing I had ever heard on the pop stations in Texas. WNOE is where I first heard Charles Brown's original version of "Please Come Home For Christmas." It always stuck with me. Our version was very much like the original.

GLENN: We were in the middle of *The Long Run* album, and we weren't going to finish anytime soon. So we cut a Christmas record in Miami. It was a fall day, by the way, and it was hot as hell. Perfect for a Christmas record.

HEARTACHE TONIGHT

GLENN: . . . and then they sold 12 million records, and everything changed! As Bob Dylan said, "They deceived me into thinking I had something to protect." And that's what happened with us. We made it, and it ate us. *The Long Run* became, indeed, the long run. It was a difficult record to make overall, but I loved "Heartache Tonight." Whenever Bob Seger was in L.A., he always used to come over and visit me, and he'd visit Don, too, and play us stuff he was working on—and we would do the same. I seem to remember that I had the verse thing going on for "Heartache Tonight," and I was showing it to Seger, and we were jammin'—I think we were jammin' on electric guitars at LaFontaine—and then he blurted out the chorus. That's how "Heartache" started. Then Bob disappeared, and J.D., Don, and I finished that song up. No heavy lyrics—the song is more of a romp—and that's what it was intended to be.

THE SAD CAFÉ

GLENN: The title comes from the book by Carson McCullers. I love the title, which didn't have anything to do with the song, other than it was a great title. The line that really resonates for me in that song is "I don't know why fortune smiles on some and lets the rest go free." There were so many of us aspiring musicians hanging around at the Troubadour. Some nights when Doug Dillard got drunk enough, and Gene Clark got drunk enough, and Harry Dean Stanton got drunk enough . . . near closing time . . . they would all start singing. There would be these unbelievable impromptu versions of "Amazing Grace"—all sorts of Ozark spiritual things with the whole bar singing. . . . That stuff really happened. We were getting older (when we wrote the song), and there was a sadness because we had seen, close-up, that everybody's dreams don't come true. Or, at least, not in the way they think they're gonna come true.

DON: A train used to run down the center of Santa Monica Boulevard, right outside the Troubadour. Steve Martin actually had a routine where he'd get the entire audience to exit the club, hop a flatcar on that slow-moving train and ride up to La Cienega, a few blocks east. Then, everybody would hop off and walk back down to the club together. I don't think that happened very many times—maybe not even more than once or twice, because the railroad people didn't like it. It was kind of dangerous and there was liability involved. Still—and I don't want to over-mythologize—it was something to remember. That was a wonderful time in Los Angeles. The city was alive with magic and a sense of possibility. People were warmer and more open than they are now.

Then, of course, there was the dark side. Friends and acquaintances of ours (from that era) had begun to meet untimely ends—classic cases of "too much, too soon." It was either that or "too little, too late." So we were struggling to make sense of that dichotomy, that contradiction. Is fortune a good thing or a bad thing, you know? Is being fortunate, before you're ready to accept it and deal with it, actually *fortunate*—or is it *unfortunate*? We were struggling with our own success—riddled with feelings of guilt and unworthiness. I think a lot of young artists feel that way. We always identified with that great song "Fakin' It," by Paul Simon. It takes many years and lots of experience for a man to get comfortable in his own skin. But the Troubadour, Dan Tana's restaurant, the train—all those things served as a great metaphor for the search, the journey that so many of us were on.

I CAN'T TELL YOU WHY

DON: Timothy came in with the title and other bits and pieces. Glenn and I just wanted to surround it with everything we could. Glenn came up with that wonderful counterpart, very much a soul-record type thing, "Try to keep your head, little girl." Glenn also composed and played that great guitar solo.

GLENN: Timothy joined the band and the real challenge, as Don and I saw it, was to get a piece of material for him that wasn't country. So we got him over to LaFontaine, and the three of us got down to work. I said, "You could sing like Smokey Robinson. Let's not do a Richie Furay, Poco-sounding song. Let's do an R&B song." He said, "Sure, love to try!" Some of those crazy moments happen when you just go over to the piano and jam. There I was, brave as a Budweiser, going right to the piano and saying, "Well, how 'bout somethin' like this?" That's another one of my absolute favorite Eagles songs. It's got the mood. It's got the "Ooh baby, baby" vocal. But, again, counterpoint—with Don and I singing against the melody and the understated, brilliant guitar stylings of yours truly [laughs]. It's another song that people love in our live show. Since it is a ballad, we are not playing too loud and can hear the audience. Timothy starts, and there are thousands of people singing, "Look at us, baby . . . "

THE LONG RUN

GLENN: We'd had the idea for about six or seven years. The title of the song was apropos, and it seemed to be a good title for the album—let's see who'll last. I think it was a lot about longevity, and it was also about me just lovin' Tyrone Davis' record "Turning Point." We had done some slicker production like the Philly sound, but "Long Run" was more like a tribute to Memphis with the slide guitars playing the parts of the horns.

DON: It was a long and difficult album. Everything was catching up to us. Too much pressure, too much worry, too much traveling, too many controlled substances, too much paranoia and infighting. I missed having a normal life. Glenn and I were starting to grow distant. Everything was pulling apart—and we were writing about longevity. [thoughtful pause] Yeah, well, even if we weren't living it, we were always able to idealize it in a song about the way we'd like to be—the way we'd like to be perceived. That song may have been a message to our critics. It may have been a message from Glenn to me or me to Glenn. It could be taken all kinds of different ways. Could be a message to a girl—a long-departed lover. But, again, it was built on that foundation of Glenn's rhythm guitar playing [sings part]. Always that foundation. So, here we are some 25 years later—32 years total—still going strong. *The Long Run*, indeed.

IN THE CITY

GLENN: Of all the songs we were considering for the album, I always loved this one of Joe's. An earlier solo version had been in the movie *The Warriors*, but it wasn't that widely known. I always liked the song and thought it could have been an Eagles record, and so we decided to make it one.

THOSE SHOES

DON: One of my favorites. At that time, all the girls were wearing Charles Jourdan shoes—the ones with the little ankle straps. They'd become very popular and we were big fans [laughs]. And so, we said, "Well, it's not enough just to write about that; we have to turn it into a metaphor for women standing on their own two feet, so to speak, and taking responsibility for their own lives, their own losses." That was our intent. The lyric "Once you've started wearing those shoes" meant "Once you've started being your own woman and taking responsibility for your own life; once you've decided not to be just decoration—an appendage to some guy—then this is all the crap you're going to have to put up with in conjunction with that." Anyone who decides to become the master of his or her own destiny always has to put up with a lot of crap. On the surface the song was about the singles scene: the beautiful, young women seemingly unaware of the sharks waiting in the shallows . . . sharks that sometimes included us. It was also a great, great beat. It gave Felder a chance to strap on the talkbox, a device which Joe Walsh pioneered on "Rocky Mountain Way"—and the two of them soloed together . . .

GLENN: As far as I know, it's the only double-talkbox solo in existence. That's Felder and Walsh on talkbox at the end singing, "Butt out . . . butt out . . . "

Photo: John Halpern

SEVEN BRIDGES ROAD

GLENN: We had heard Ian Matthews, from Matthews' Southern Comfort, and he'd recorded that song on his album. We listened to his version and then modified our arrangement from that. Sometimes we start our show with it. It's something we do well—four voices, a cappella. I think the bottom line is, that's a style that comes very easily and naturally to us. It's also something that our fans really love. It's Americana.

LOVE WILL KEEP US ALIVE

GLENN: There was a short time, while the band had broken up, that Timothy and Sharkey—that's Felder—were trying to put together a group with Max Carl from Jack Mack And The Heart Attack, Jim Capaldi from Traffic, and Paul Carrack. The five of them were getting together, I believe, out at Felder's house and doing demos, trying to write songs and sing and do different things. From those demo sessions came Paul Carrack singing "Love Will Keep Us Alive."

GET OVER IT

DON: Written in a burst. It's the fastest song, tempo-wise, that we've ever recorded. The best thing about it is that it got Glenn and I in a room together again, after 14 years, and we created something as a team, even if it wasn't the best thing we ever wrote.

GLENN: We were so sick of tabloid television—and this was *eight years ago*! I was so tired of professional victims everywhere you looked, all over the media. Don said, "I have a title: 'Get Over It.'" I said, "That's a song—let's write it!" We got together at his place up the coast and wrote it. Whether it's the best song we've ever written or not, it was the song that proved to us that we could write together again. During *The Long Run* our creative relationship became strained, perhaps just because we'd been going to the well for so long. We struggled to complete all the songs for *The Long Run* album. Let's just say that I was less than confident that Don and I could get back in a room together and get through a piece of work. "Get Over It" showed us that we could get together and write again. For that reason it's an important song to me.

HOLE IN THE WORLD

GLENN: We were supposed to start our record. We loaded in on Monday, September 10, to start the Eagles studio album in earnest. All the equipment was put in the day before, and we were supposed to go to the studio on the morning of 9/11, but after hearing the news we called each other up and said, "What's the point? I don't think there's anything worth showing up for today." So we stayed home. And then that night Don started "Hole In The World."

DON: On September 10, 2001, my bandmates and I were still feeling elated from the successful tour of Europe we had completed in August. We had traveled all over the continent and made first-ever appearances in Russia, Finland, and Italy. It had been a memorable, satisfying experience. We were back in L.A. and preparing to record. Then, on the morning of September 11, the phone rang and it was my assistant, who said, "You'd better turn on the TV." That evening, our recording session having been cancelled, I sat down at the piano in my home studio and started putting some chords with the phrase "hole in the world." Just sort of wrote the refrain in one sitting. After that, the first verse came fairly quickly and then I was stuck. Months went by, but I didn't show it to anybody. Then, other things started happening that gave additional meanings to "Hole In The World," particularly after the [Iraqi] war started. The fighting was supposedly over in May, and yet one or two or three of our boys were—and still are—getting killed every day, which means somebody's daddy is not coming home. So that's another "hole"—a huge hole in somebody's life—a child, a wife, a mother, a father, a brother, a sister. There are holes in the information that the public is getting, both from the media and the government. There are holes in what passes for the logic of this administration's foreign policy. The stars and stripes may be flying and the drums beating, but things are never going to be the same for some people. The ill-conceived attempt to "avenge" the victims of September 11 has only brought more misery and sorrow. Things in today's world are not so black-and-white, so clear-cut. This is not a John Wayne movie. This is the 21st century. It's complex, and people have forgotten about our history—if they ever really knew it in the first place.

So I took my unfinished piece to the studio and showed it to Glenn, and he eventually wrote the second verse. We started a third verse and then scrapped it in favor of simplicity. I originally envisioned it as a very short song, anyway, like those little snippets The Beatles used to do that only lasted for about a minute, but it turned out to be a little longer than that.

GLENN: Talk about a record that you know is the Eagles: "Hi, we're in charge again." These would be the compelling perfect vocals, and of course let's just start with Don's opening lines of the song, which I think are brilliant—"They say that anger is just love disappointed." It's all there. The big chorus, the *oooh*s under the first verse. . . . It's a classic Eagles record, I'm telling you.

DON: A lot has happened since that summer of 1971. It is amazing and gratifying that so many people, all over the world, still love these songs and come out in droves to hear us play them. I live in Texas now, and sometimes, late at night, when I'm pushing the cart around the supermarket, I'll hear one of our records and I think, "I left here 33 years ago, did all that, and here I am back again . . . now, what did I come here to buy?"

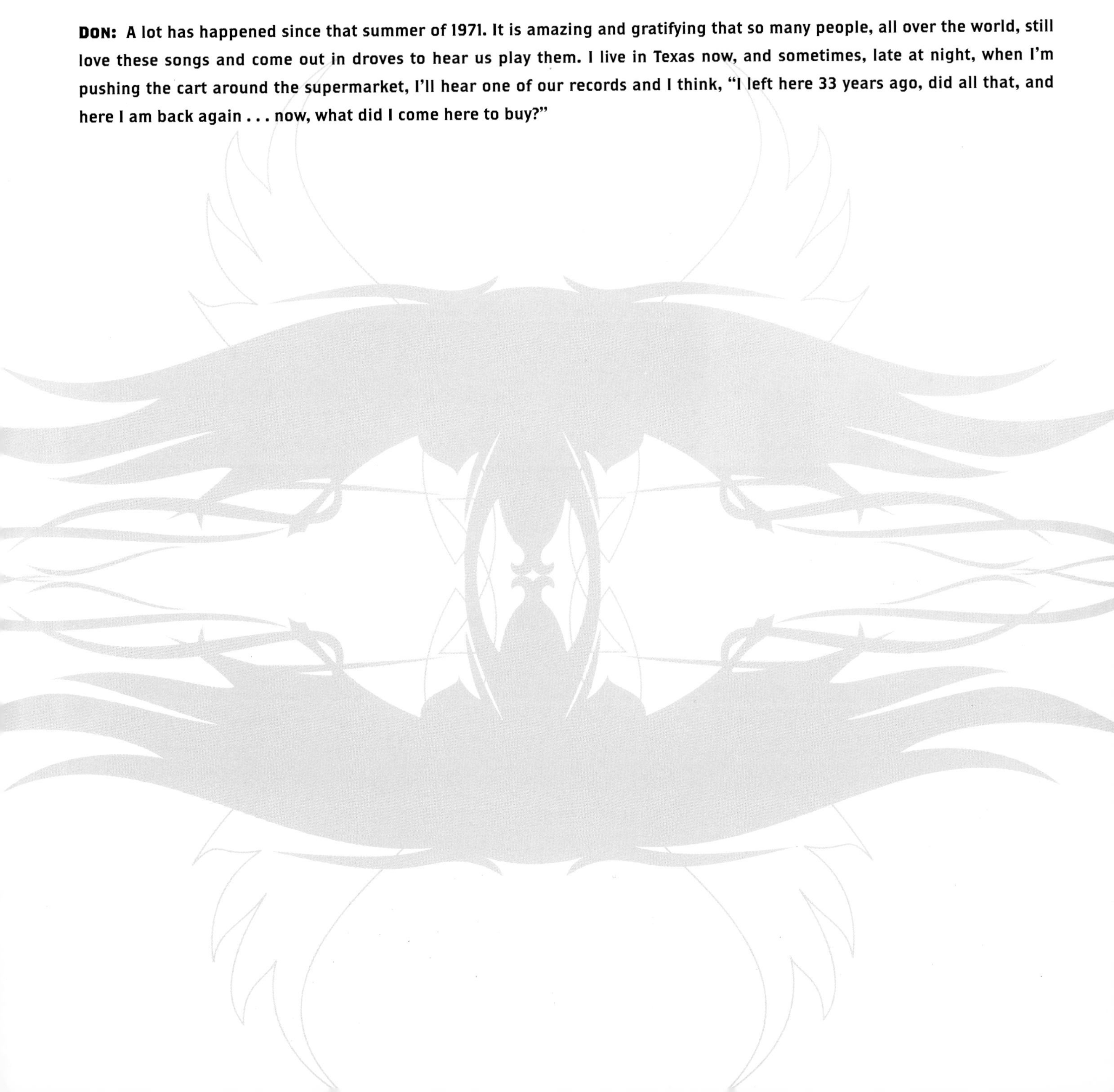

Photo: James R. Minchin III

DISC 1

AFTER THE THRILL IS GONE

Words and Music by
DON HENLEY and GLENN FREY

C
Am
G
fro - zen pen;
you're not quite lov - ers and you're not quite friends
twice as long;
so you keep on sing - ing for the sake of the song
steps you choose;
you don't care a - bout win - ning but you don't want to lose
Am
G
To Coda
af - ter the thrill is gone, oh,
af - ter the thrill is gone.
af - ter the thrill is gone,
af - ter the thrill is gone.
af - ter the thrill is gone,
G
G/F♯
Em
Bm7
What can you do when your dreams come true and it's
You're a - fraid you might fall out of fash - ion and you're

Am7
G
Em
Bm7
not quite like you planned?
What have you done to be los - ing the one, you
feel - ing cold and small.
An - y kind of love with-out pas - sion, that ain't
Cm6
1. D7sus4
2. D7sus4
D7 D. S. al Coda
held it so tight in your hand,
well.
well.
no kind of lov - ing at all,
Coda
Am
G
Am
G
af - ter the thrill is gone,
af - ter the thrill is gone,
oh,
Cm6
G
C
Cm6
G
af - ter the thrill is gone.

TAKE IT EASY

Words and Music by
JACKSON BROWNE and GLENN FREY

G
Em
C
Take it eas - y, take it eas -
G
Am
C
Em
y, don't let the sound of your own wheels drive you cra - zy.
C
G
C
Light-en up while you still can, don't e-ven try to un-der-stand,
G
Am
C
G
just find a place to make your stand and take it eas -

G
xooo
y.
Well, I'm a - stand-in' on a cor-ner in Wins-
D
C
low, Ar - i - zo - na and such a fine sight to see, it's a girl,
G
xooo
D
C
my Lord, in a flat bed Ford slow-in' down to take a look at me.
G
xooo
Em
D
C
Come on, ba - by, don't say may - be,

G
Am
C
Em
I got-ta know if your sweet love is gon-na save me.
C
G
C
We may lose and we may win, though we will nev-er be here a-gain,
G
Am
C
G
so o-pen up, I'm climb-in' in, so take it eas -
G
y. Well, I'm a - run-nin' down the road try'n' to loos-en my load, got a world

D
Am7
G
of trou - ble on my mind,
look - in' for a lov - er who won't
C
Em
blow my cov - er, she's so hard to find.
Take it eas - y,
take it eas - y,
don't let the sound of your own
Am
wheels make you cra - zy.
Come on, ba - by,

G
C
G
Am
don't_ say_ may - be, I ___ got-ta know if your_ sweet_love_
C
G
Tacet
C
G
___ is gon-na save ___ me. __
C
G
G9
C
Oh,_ we got it eas - y, ___
G
G9
C
Em
we ought-a take it eas - y. ___
R. H.

WITCHY WOMAN

Words and Music by
BERNIE LEADON and DON HENLEY

Gm
3 fr.
D7
Woo - hoo, witch-y wom - an, See how high she flies.
Woo - hoo, witch-y wom - an, She got the moon in her eyes.
B♭
F
D
C
To Coda
She
held me spell-bound in the night, Danc - ing shad-ows and fire - light,

D7
Gm
3 fr.
D.S.
al Coda
Cra - zy laugh-ter in an - oth - er room_ And she drove her-self_to mad-ness with a sil - ver spoon._
Coda
C
Gm
Dm7
Ah
ah
1. Gm
2. Gm
I know_ you want to love her, but let me tell you, broth-er, She's been
Cm
B♭
sleep - in' in the dev - il's bed._ There's some ru - mors go - in' 'round,_

Bb
C
Gm
3 fr.
Some-one's un-der-ground, She can rock you in_ the night un-til your skin turn red._
Gm
3 fr.
D7
Gm
3 fr.
Woo - hoo, witch-y wom-an, See how high_ she flies._
D7
Woo - hoo, witch-y wom - an, She got the moon_ in her eyes._
Gm
3 fr.
F
D
C
D
C
Gm
3 fr.
C
Gm
3 fr.
F
Gm
3 fr.
rit.
R. H.

PEACEFUL EASY FEELING

Words and Music by
JACK TEMPCHIN

A
E
A
B
Bsus4
2 fr.
B
with a bil - lion stars all_ a-round.
'Cause I got a
A
E
A
peace - ful
eas - y feel - in',
and I know you won't_
F#m7
B
E
F#m7
A
let me_ down,
'cause I'm al - read-y stand - in'
Bsus4
2 fr.
E
Esus4
E
Esus4
on the ground.

E
A
And I found out a long_ time ___ a - go ___
what a wom-an can do ___ to your_ soul, ___
B
Bsus4
2 fr.
ah, but she ___ can't take you_ an - y - way, ___
you don't al-read-y know ___ how_ to go. ___ And I got a

A
E
peace - ful easy - y feel - in',
A
Bsus4
2 fr.
B
and I know you won't let me down,
'cause I'm
E
F♯m7
A
To Coda
Bsus4
2 fr.
al - read-y stand - in' on the ground.
E
Esus4
E
Esus4

E
A
E
A
I get this feel - in' I may know you
E
A
B
as a lov - er and a friend,
E
A
E
A
but this voice keeps whis - per - ing in my oth - er ear, tells me
D.S. 𝄋 al Coda ⊕
E
A
B
Bsus4
2 fr.
B
I may nev - er see you a - gain.
'Cause I get a

Coda
Bsus4
2 fr.
E
F#m7
A
I'm — al - read-y stand-in', yes, I'm — al - read-y stand-in' on the ground.
B
Whoa.
rit.

DESPERADO

Words and Music by
DON HENLEY and GLENN FREY

A7
D7
G
Gsus4 sus2
so long now.
Oh, you're a hard one,
I know that
C
Cm6
G/D
B/D#
Em7
you got your rea - sons,
these things that are pleas - in' you
can
A7
D7
G
D/F#
Em
Bm7
hurt you some-how.
Don't you draw the queen of dia -monds, boy, she'll
mf
C
G
G/F#
Em7
C
beat you if she's a - ble,
you know the queen of hearts is al - ways your best bet.

G
D/F#
Em
Bm7
Now it seems to me some fine things have been
C
G
Em
A7
laid up-on your ta - ble, but you on - ly want the ones that you can't get.
Am7/D
D
D7
G
Dm7/G
Des - per - a - do, oh, you ain't
C
Bm
Am
G
D/F#
Em
get-tin' no young - er, your pain and your hun - ger, they're

A7 D7 G Dm7/G
driv-in' you home. And free-dom, oh, free-dom, well, that's just
C Bm Am G B7/F# Em
some peo-ple talk-in', your pris-on is walk-in' through this
A7 D7 G D/F# Em Bm7
world all a-lone. Don't your feet get cold in the win-ter time? The
C G D/F# Em C
sky won't snow and the sun won't shine, it's hard to tell the night-time from the

G
D/F#
Em
Bm7
day. You're los - in' all your highs and lows. Ain't it
C
G
Am7
fun - ny how the feel - in' goes a - way?
Am7/D
D
D7
G
Dm7
Des - per - a - do, why don't you
C
Cm6
G
D/F#
Em
come to your sens - es? Come down from your fenc - es,

A7
D7
G
Dm7
o - pen the gate. It may be rain - in', but there's a
C
Cm6
G
B7/F#
Em
rain - bow a - bove you. You bet - ter let some - bod - y love you,
C
G/B
Am
G/D
B7/D#
Em
you bet - ter let some - bod - y love you be -
Am7/D
G
G7
C
Cm6
G
fore it's too late.
mp
rit.

TEQUILA SUNRISE

Words and Music by
DON HENLEY and GLENN FREY

Gmaj7
G6
G
D
He was just a hired hand work-in' on the
Am
D7
G
Gmaj7
dreams he planned to try,
the days go by.
G6
G
Em
C
Em
Ev-'ry night when the sun goes down,
just an-oth-er
C
Em
Am
D7
G/D
lone-ly boy in town,
and she's out run-nin' 'round.

G
D
She was-n't just an-oth-er wom-an and I could-n't
Am
D7
G
G6
keep from com-in' on, it's been so long.
Oh, and it's a hol-low feel-in', when it comes
down to deal-in' friends, it nev-er ends.

G
D
Am7
D
G
R. H.
Am
D
Bm
Take an - oth - er shot of cour - age, won - der why the
E
Am
B
right words nev - er come, you just get numb.

Em7
A
G
It's an - oth - er te - qui -
D
Am
la sun - rise, this old world still looks the same,
D7
G
G6
Gmaj7
G6
G
Gmaj7
an - oth - er frame.
G6
G
Gmaj7
G6
G
G6
(Mm.)

THE BEST OF MY LOVE

Words and Music by
DON HENLEY, GLENN FREY
and JOHN DAVID SOUTHER

Dm
Em
com-in' a-part at the seams.
left us so lit-tle to give.
We try to talk it o-
That same old crowd was like a
Dm
Em
ver but the words come out too rough;
cold dark cloud that we could nev-er rise a-bove;
F/G
C
Dm
I know you were try-in' to give me the best of your
but here in my heart I give you the best of my
C
1.
G7
2.
G7
C
love.
love.
Oh, sweet dar-

Dm
lin', you get the best of my love, oh,
C
sweet dar - lin',
Dm
you get the best of my
love.
Fm7
I'm go - in' back in time and it's a
C
sweet dream;
Fm7
it was a qui - et night and I would

Dm
G7
be all right if I could go on sleep - ing. But
C
ev - 'ry morn - in' I wake up and wor - ry
Dm
C
what's gon-na hap-pen to - day;
you see it your way, and
Dm
I see it mine, but we both see it slip-pin' a - way.

Em
Dm
Em
You know we al-ways had each oth-er, ba - by, I guess that was-n't e-nough;
Dm
G7
C
oh, but here in my heart I
Dm
C
G7
give you the best of my love. Oh,
Repeat and fade
C
Dm
sweet dar - lin', you get the best of my love. Oh,
Repeat and fade

DOOLIN–DALTON

Words and Music by
GLENN FREY, JOHN DAVID SOUTHER,
DON HENLEY and JACKSON BROWNE

A
E
F#m
They were duel - in', Doo-lin - Dal-
A
F#m
ton, high or low, it was the same.
A
A7
D
Eas - y mon-ey and faith - less
F#m
B
D
A
C#
4 fr.
wom-en, red-eye whis - key for the pain.

F#m
A
C#
4 fr.
F#m
Go down, Bill_Dal-ton, it must be God's will,_
two broth-ers_ ly - in' dead_in
A
A7
D
F#m
Cof-fey - ville._
Two voic-es call_ to you from where they stood,
B
D
A
C#m
4 fr.
lay down your_ law - books now, they're no damn good._ Bet-ter keep on
F#m
A
C#m
4 fr.
mov - in',_
Doo - lin - Dal - ton,_
'til your

F♯m
A
A7
shad - ow
sets you
free.
If you're fast
D
F♯m
and if you're
luck-y,
you will
B
D
A
nev - er
see that hang - in'
tree.
Well, the
C♯m
4 fr.
A
D
towns lay out a - cross
the dust - y plains
like grave-

Bm
F#m
yards filled with tomb - stones
wait - in' for the names. —
And a
A
Em7
A7
D
man could use his back — or use — his brains,
but some —
Bm
E
C#
4 fr.
— just went stir cra - zy, Lord, — 'cause noth - in' ev - er changed — 'til Bill —
F#m
A
Doo - lin met Bill Dal - ton. —
He was work - in' cheap, —

F♯m
A
A7
just bid - in' time.
Then he laughed
D
F♯m
and said, "I'm go - in',"
and so he
B
E
A
E
left that peace - ful life be - hind.
F♯m
A7
D
C♯m
4 fr.
Bm
E
D
F♯
(Mm.
)

ALREADY GONE

Words and Music by
JACK TEMPCHIN and
ROBB STRANDLUND

C
G
But let me tell you I got some news for you
Just re-mem-ber this,
D
C
and you'll soon find out it's true,
and then you'll
my girl, when you look up in the sky
you can
G
D
C
have to eat your lunch all by your-self.
see the stars and still not see the light.
G
D
C
'Cause I'm
And I'm
al-read-y gone,

G
x000
D
0
C
0 0
and I'm feel - in' strong,
G
x000
D
0
To Coda
I will sing this vic - t'ry song,
C
0 0
G
x000
D
0
woo, hoo, hoo,
woo, hoo, hoo.
1.
C
0 0
The
2.
C
0 0
Well, I

G
D
C
know it was - n't you who held me down;
G
D
heav-en knows it was - n't you who set me free.
C
G
D
So of-ten - times it hap - pens that we
C
G
live our lives in chains and we nev - er e - ven know

D
C
D. S. 𝄋 al Coda 𝄌
we have the key.
But me, I'm al -
Coda
C
G
'cause I'm al -
D
C
read - y gone.
Yes, I'm al -
G
F
read - y gone,
and I'm feel -

C
G
F
in' strong,
I will sing
this vic - t'ry song,
'cause I'm al -
read - y gone.
Repeat and fade
Al - read - y gone.
Repeat and fade

JAMES DEAN

Words and Music by
JACKSON BROWNE, JOHN DAVID SOUTHER,
DON HENLEY and GLENN FREY

Moderately fast Rock beat

A
you said it all so clean, and I
E
know my life would look all right if I could see it on the sil - ver screen.
A
A
You were the low down reb - el if there
ev - er was, e - ven if you had no cause. James

D
A
Dean,
you said it all _ so clean, _
E
_ and I know my life _ would look all right _ if I could
A
see it on the sil - ver screen. _
We'll
D
A
talk a - bout a low-down bad _ re - frig - er - a - tor, you were just too cool _ for school. _

D
Sock hop, so - da pop, bas-ket-ball and au - to shop, the
B
E
A
on - ly thing that got you off was break-in' all the rules._ James Dean, James
Dean, so hun - gry_ and_ so_ lean._ James
D
A
Dean, you said it all_ so clean,_

E
and I know my life would look all right if I could
A
see it on the sil - ver screen.
D
Lit-tle James Dean up on the screen
A
won-d'rin' who he might be;
D
a - long came a Spy - der, picked up a ri - der,

B
E
A
took him down the road to e - ter - ni - ty. James Dean, James
Dean, you bought it sight un - seen. James
D
A
Dean, James Dean, you bought it sight un - seen.
E
You were too fast to live, too young to die, bye -

A
E
bye;
you were too fast to live, _
D
too young to die, _ bye - bye. _
Bye -
A
B/A
bye, _
bye - bye, _
bye - bye, _
D/A
F/A
A6
bye - bye. _

OL' 55

Words and Music by
TOM WAITS

OI' 55 - 5 - 1

F
F/G
G7
C
Em7
knows_ I was feel-in' a - live. And now the sun's com-in' up,
mf
To Coda
I'm rid-in' with La - dy Luck,
Dm
G
Em
free-way cars and trucks.
Stars be - gin-ning to fade,
Am
and I lead the pa - rade;

Dm
G
Am
just a - wish - in' I'd stayed a lit - tle long - er,
D
F/G
G7
Lord, don't you know the feel - in's get - tin' strong - er.
C
Em7
F
F/G
Six in the morn - in, gave me no warn - in', I had to be on my
mp
C
G9
C
Em7
way. Now the cars are all pass - in' me, trucks are all flash - in' me,

F F/G G7
I'm head - ed home from your place. And now the
C Em7 F F/G G7 C Em7
sun's com-in' up, I'm rid-in' with La - dy Luck,
mf
F F/G G7 C Em
free-way cars and trucks.
F Em Dm G C Am
Stars be - gin-ning to fade,

Dm
G
C
Am
Dm
G
and I lead the pa - rade;
just a - wish-in' I'd stayed
Am
D
a lit - tle long - er,
Lord, don't you know the
F/G
G7
F/G
G7
D. S. al Coda
Coda
Repeat and fade
C
Em7
feel - in's get-tin' strong - er
Well, my
Free-way cars and trucks,
mp
Repeat and fade
F
F/G
G7
C
Em7
F
F/G
G7
rid-in' with La - dy Luck.

MIDNIGHT FLYER

Bright Country style

Words and Music by
PAUL CRAFT

Midnight Flyer - 4 - 1

G
D
Oo, Mid-night Fly - er,
Bm
Em
A
D
I paid my dues and I feel like trav-'lin' on.
A
D
G
D
G
run-a-way team of hors-es ain't e-nough to make me stay, so throw your rope on an-
May-be I'll go to San-ta Fe, may-be San An-tone; an-y town is
A
D
oth-er man and pull him down your way. Make him in-to some-
where I'm bound any way to get me gone. Don't think a-bout

G
D
Bm
Em
one to take the place of me,
— me, never let me cross your mind,
make him ev - 'ry
'cept when you
kind of fool you want - ed me to be.
hear that mid - night lone - some whis - tle whine.
A
D
G
Oo,
Mid-night Fly - er,
D
G
en - gi - neer, won't you let your whis - tle moan?
D

G
Oo, Mid-night
D
Bm
Em
A
Fly - er, I paid my dues and I feel like trav-'lin' on,
D
Bm
Em
A
I paid my dues and I feel like trav-'lin' on.
C
G
D

ON THE BORDER

Words and Music by
BERNIE LEADON, DON HENLEY
and GLENN FREY

E
G
A
G
E
B
"Son, you bet-ter get on one side or the oth - er.
I'm
A
E
B
A
E
B
out on the bor - der,
I'm walk-in' the line.
Don't you tell me 'bout your
A
E
B
A
E
law and or - der,
I'm try'n' to change this
wa - ter to wine.
A
E
A
E
A
E
E
G
A
Af - ter a hard day I'm

C
E
G
A
C
safe at home,
fool-in' with my ba-by on the tel - e-phone;
E
G
A
C
Tacet
(Spoken)
(Sung)
out of no-where some-bod-y cuts in and says,
"Hmm, you in some trou-ble, boy, we
A
G
E
B
A
E
know where you been."
I'm out on the bor - der,
I'm stuck on the bor - der,
B
A
E
B
I thought this was a pri-vate line.
all I want-ed was some peace of mind.
Don't you tell me 'bout your

A
E
B
To Coda
A
E
law and_ or - der,
I'm try'n' to change this_
wa-ter to wine.___
E
Nev-er mind your_ name,_____
just give us your num - ber,
mm;_____
simile
nev-er mind your face, _
just show us your card, _
mm. _
And we wan-na know_____
whose wing are you un -

der;
you bet-ter step to the right
or we can make it hard.
D. S. 𝄋 al Coda
Coda
A
E
wa-ter to wine.
On the bor-
Repeat and fade
E
G
A
der,
on the bor - der.
On the bor-
Repeat and fade

TAKE IT TO THE LIMIT

Words and Music by
DON HENLEY, GLENN FREY
and RANDY MEISNER

G/D
C
F
al - ways been a dream - er (spent my life run-ning 'round), and it's so hard to
look - ing for your free - dom (no - bod - y seems to care), and you can't find the
change (can't seem to set - tle down); but the dreams I've seen
door (can't find it an - y - where), when there's noth - ing to be -
Dm
F/G
late - ly keep on turn - ing out and burn - ing out and
lieve in still you're com - ing back, you're run - ning back, you're
G
turn - ing out the same.
com - ing back for more.
So put me on a high - way and

F
C
F
Tacet
G
1. C
show me a sign, and take it to the lim - it one more time.
G
F
2. Am
G
You can time.
Repeat and fade
F
G
F
G
Take it to the lim - it, take it to the lim - it,
Repeat and fade
F
Tacet
G
Tacet
C
take it to the lim - it one more time.

ONE OF THESE NIGHTS

Words and Music by
DON HENLEY and GLENN FREY

Bm
Em
Em/D
The full moon is call - ing, the fe - ver is high and the
I've been search-ing for the daugh - ter of the dev - il him - self; I've been
Cmaj7
Am
wick - ed wind whis - pers and moans.
search - ing for an an - gel in white.
You got your de - mons,
I've been wait - ing for a wom - an who's a
Em
Bm7
you got de - sires; well, I got a few of my own.
lit - tle of both, and I can feel her but she's no - where in sight.

Cmaj7
Gmaj7
Oo, some-one to be kind to in be-tween the dark and the light;
Oo, lone-li-ness will blind you in be-tween the wrong and the right;
Cmaj7
oo, com-ing right be-hind you,
oo, com-ing right be-hind you,
Am
1.Bm
No chord
2.Bm
N. C.
swear I'm gon-na find you one of these nights. One of these
swear I'm gon-na find you one of these nights. One of these

Cmaj7
Gmaj7
nights, in be-tween the dark and the light;
Cmaj7
com-ing right be-hind you, swear I'm gon-na find you,
Gmaj7
Repeat and fade (vocal ad lib)
Cmaj7
get you, ba-by, one of these nights. One of these nights.
Repeat and fade
Gmaj7
One of these

LYIN' EYES

Words and Music by
DON HENLEY and GLENN FREY

C
Am
C
ry;
she'll dress up all in lace__ and go in style.__
__ one;
she draws the shade and hangs__ her head to cry.__
G
Gmaj7
Late at night__ a big old house__ gets lone-
On the oth-er side__ of town a boy__ is wait-
She won-ders how__ it ev-er got__ this cra-
C
Am
ly;
I guess ev-'ry form__ of ref-uge has its price.__
ing
with fi-ery eyes__ and dreams no one could steal.__
zy;
she thinks a-bout__ a boy she knew in school.__

D
G
Gmaj7
And it breaks her heart to think her love is on-
She drives on through the night an - tic - i - pat-
Did she get tired or did she just get la-
C
Am
C
ly giv - en to a man with hands as cold as ice.
ing, 'cause he makes her feel the way she used to feel.
zy? She's so far gone she feels just like a fool.
G
C
D
G
Gmaj7
So she tells him she must go out for the eve-
She rush - es to his arms, they fall to - geth-
My, oh my, you sure know how to ar-

C
Am
ning
to com-fort an old friend who's feel-in' down.
er;
she whis-pers that it's on - ly for a while.
range things;
you set it up so well, so care-ful-ly.
D
G
Gmaj7
But he knows where she's go - in' as she's
She swears that soon she'll be com - in' 'back for
Ain't it fun-ny how your new life did - n't
C
Am
C
leav - in';
she is head-ed for the cheat-in' side of town.
ev - er;
she pulls a - way and leaves him with a smile.
change things;
you're still the same old girl you used to be.

G
G
C/G
You can't hide your ly - in' eyes,
G
Em
Bm
and your smile is a thin dis -
Am
D
G
G9
guise. I thought by now you'd re - al - ize
C
A
Am
D
To Coda
there ain't no way to hide your ly - in' eyes.

1. G
2. G
D. S. al Coda
Coda G
Gmaj7
Am
D
There ain't no way to hide your ly - in' eyes.
G
Gmaj7
Am
D
G
Hon-ey, you can't hide your ly - in' eyes.
Gmaj7
Am
D
G
rit.

HOTEL CALIFORNIA

Words and Music by
DON HENLEY, GLENN FREY
and DON FELDER

A
hair, warm_ smell of co - li - tas__
bends. She got a lot of pret - ty, pret - ty boys_
E
rls - ing up through the air.___
that she calls friends.___
G
Up a - head in the
How they dance in the
D
dis - tance, I saw a shim - mer - ing light.
court - yard; sweet sum - mer sweat.
Em
My head grew heav - y and my sight grew dim;___
Some dance to re - mem - ber;___

F♯
Bm
I had to stop for the night.
some dance to for - get.
There she stood in the
So I called up the
F♯
door - way;
cap - tain:
I heard the mis - sion bell.
"Please bring me my wine."
He said,
A
And I was think - ing to my - self:
this could be
"We have - n't had that spir - it here
since
E
G
heav - en or this could be hell.
nine - teen six - ty - nine."
Then she lit up a
And still those

D
Em
F♯
G
D
F♯
can - dle, and she showed me the way.
voic-es are call - ing from far a - way;
There were voic-es down the cor - ri - dor;_ I thought I heard them
wake you up in the mid-dle of the night just to hear them
say:_ "Wel - come_ to the Ho - tel Cal - i - for-
say:_ "Wel - come_ to the Ho - tel Cal - i - for-
nia. Such a love - ly place,_ (such a
nia. Such a love - ly place,_ (such a

Bm
love - ly place_) such a love - ly face._
love - ly place_) such a love - ly face._
G
x000
Plen - ty of room_ at the Ho - tel Cal - i - for -
They liv - in' it up_ at the Ho - tel Cal - i - for -
D
0
Em
0 000
nia. An - y time_ of year,_ (an - y
nia. What a nice_ sur - prise;_ (what a
1. F#
time_ of year_) you can find_ it here."_
nice_ sur - prise_) bring your

2.
F♯
Bm
al - i - bis."
Mir - rors on the ceil - ing, the pink cham - pagne on ice, and she said, "We are all just pris - on - ers here of our own de - vice."
Last thing I re - mem - ber, I was run - ning for the door. I had to find the pas - sage back to the place I was be - fore.
F♯
A
E

G
And in the mas - ter's chamb - bers,
"Re - lax," said the night man. "We are
D
they gath - ered for the feast.
pro - gramed to re - ceive.
Em
They stab it with their steel - y knives, but they
You can check out an - y time you like, but
F#
1.
2.
D. C. and fade
just can't kill the beast.
leave."
you can nev - er

DISC 2

LIFE IN THE FAST LANE

Words and Music by
DON HENLEY, GLENN FREY
and JOE WALSH

E
hard-head-ed man.___ He was bru - tal - ly hand - some, and she was ter-mi-nal - ly pret-ty.
Ea - ger for ac - tion and hot for the game,_ the com-ing at - trac - tion, the
She held him up, and he held her for ran - som in the heart_
drop of a name._ They knew all the right peo-ple; they took all the right pills.___ They threw
A7
of the cold, cold___ cit - y. He had a nas - ty rep - u - ta - tion as a
out - ra - geous par-ties; they paid heav - i - ly bills. There were lines on the mir - ror,

E
cru - el dude.___ They said he was ruth - less; they said he was crude.___ They had
lines on her face. She pre - tend-ed not to no-tice; she was caught up in the__ race.
B7
A7
one thing in com - mon: they were good in bed.___ She'd say, "Fast - er, fas - ter. The
Out ev - 'ry eve - ning un - til it was light, he was too tired to make_ it; she was
E
tacet
lights are turn - in' red."______
too tired to fight a - bout it.
Life in the fast__ lane

E
tacet
sure - ly make_ you lose_ your mind.___
E
tacet
Life in the fast_ lane.
1.
E
tacet
Mm.____
E
Are you with me so far?

2.
E
tacet
E
tacet
Life in the fast lane;
E
tacet
E
tacet
ev - 'ry - thing all the time.
Life in the fast lane, uh
To Coda
E
tacet
B7
huh.
D
B7

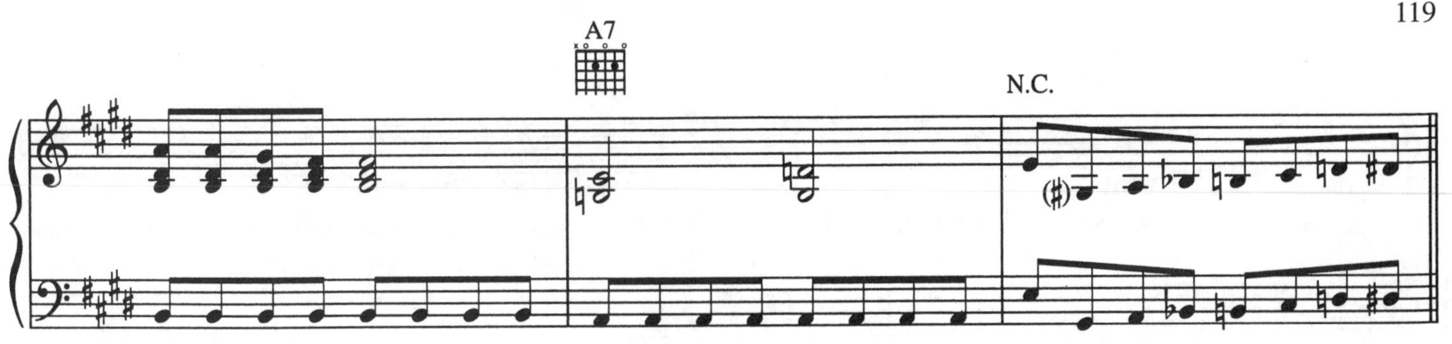
A7
N.C.

E
Blow-in' and burn - in', blind-ed by thirst,_ they___ did-n't see the stop_ sign; took a turn_

for the worst. She said, "Lis - ten, ba-by. You can hear the en - gine ring. We've been
A7
up and down this high-way; have-n't seen a god - dam thing." He said, "Call the doc - tor. I
E
think I'm gon - na crash." "The doc - tor say he's com - in', but you
B7
got - ta pay him cash." They went rush - in' down that free - way; messed a -
3

A7
D.S. 𝄋 (no repeats) al Coda
round and got lost.
They did - n't know they were just dy - in' to get off. And it was
Coda
E
D/E
Life in the fast lane.
C/E
A/E
Life in the fast lane.
E
Repeat and fade

WASTED TIME

Words and Music by
DON HENLEY and GLENN FREY

F
C/E
Dm
F/G
G7
ba - by's gone, and you're all a - lone, and it looks like the end.
don't care much for a stran-ger's touch, but you can't hold your man.
Am
E/G♯
G
D/F♯
You nev-er thought you'd be a - lone this far down the line. And
F
Em
Dm
F/G
G7
I know what's been on your mind. You're a - fraid it's all been wast - ed
C
Bm7
E7
Am
time. The au-tumn leaves have got you think-ing

Bm7
E7
Am
a-bout the first time that you fell.
Bm7
E7
Am
C/G
You did-n't love the boy too much. No, no, you just
F
C/G
Fm6/D
F/G
G
G7
C
loved the boy too well. Fare-well. So you live from day to
Fm6
C/G
F/G
G
day, and you dream a-bout to-mor-row, oh. And the

F
C/E
Dm
C/E
hours go by like min-utes, and the shad-ows come to stay. So ya
F
C/E
Dm
G7
G♯o7
take a lit-tle some-thing to make them go a-way.
Am
E/G♯
G
D/F♯
And I could have done so man-y things, ba-by, if I could on-ly stop my mind from
F
Em
Dm
F/G
G7
won-d'rin' what I left be-hind and from wor-ry-in' 'bout this wast-ed

C
Ab
4 fr.
C
time.
Ooh, an-oth-er love has come and gone.
Ab
4 fr.
C
Ooh, and the years keep rush-ing on.
I re-
F
C/E
Dm
C/E
mem-ber what you told me before you went out on your own:
"Some-times to
F
C/E
Dm
G7
G#o7
keep it to-geth-er, we got to leave it a-lone."
So

Am E/G♯ G D/F♯
you can get on with your search, ba - by, and I can get on with mine. And
F Em Dm F/G G7
may-be some-day we will find that it was-n't real - ly wast - ed
C C/E F C/G A♭ 4 fr. C C/E F C/G
time. Mm, hm, mm. Oh,
A♭ 4 fr. C C/E F C/G A♭ 4 fr. Fm6 C
hoo, ooh, ooh. Ooh, ooh, mm.
molto rit.
8va bassa

VICTIM OF LOVE

Words and Music by
DON FELDER, DON HENLEY,
JOHN DAVID SOUTHER and GLENN FREY

Moderate Rock beat

Gm 3 fr. C Gm 3 fr.

still make you thirst - y and hot. I
look - in' for love in be - tween.

heard a - bout you and that man. C There's just
Tell me your se - crets; I'll tell you mine.

Gm 3 fr. B♭ A

one thing I don't un - der - stand. You
This ain't no time to be cool. And

Gm 3 fr. C

say he's a liar and he put out your fire. How come you
tell all your girl - friends, your "been a - round the world" friends that

Gm
3 fr.
C
Gm
3 fr.
F
Gm7
F/A
still got his gun in your hand?
talk is for los - ers and fools.
B♭
Gm
3 fr.
Vic - tim of love, I see a bro - ken heart.
Vic - tim of love, I see a bro - ken heart.
Vic - tim of love, you're just a vic - tim of love.
C
B♭
F
Gm7
F/A
3
You got your sto - ries to tell.
I could be wrong, but I'm not.
I could be wrong, but I'm not.
B♭
Gm
3 fr.
Vic - tim of love, it's such an eas - y part. And
Vic - tim of love, we're not so far a - part. Show me,
Vic - tim of love, now you're a vic - tim of love.

1.
Eb
F
To Coda
Gm
3 fr.
you know how to play it so well.
what kind of love have you got?
What kind of love have you got?
2.
Gm
F
Gm7
F/A
D. S. al Coda
Coda
What kind of love have you got?
What kind of love have you got?
rit. e dim.

THE LAST RESORT

Words and Music by
DON HENLEY and GLENN FREY

B
E
A
like a ref-u - gee,_
just as_ her fa - ther came_
Esus4
a-cross_ the sea._
She heard_ a-bout_ a place_
Then the chill - y winds blew down_
mf - mf
peo-ple_ were_ smil - in'.
a-cross_ the_ des - ert,
They spoke a-bout the red_man's way,_
through the can-yons of_ the coast,_
how_ they loved_ the land._
to_ the Mal - i - bu,_
And they came from ev-'ry-where,_
where the pret-ty peo-ple play,_

B
E
A
to the Great Di - vide,
seek-ing a place to stand
hun - gry for pow - er,
to light their ne - on way
B
E
E sus4
E
A
or a place to hide.
Down in the crowd-ed bars,
and give them things to do.
Some rich men came and raped the land;
B
E
A
out for a good time,
can't wait to tell you all
no - bod - y caught 'em.
Put up a bunch of ug - ly box - es,
B
E
A
what it's like up there.
And they called it par - a - dise.
and Je - sus, peo - ple bought 'em.
And they called it par - a - dise,

B
E
A
I don't_ know_ why.
the place_ to___ be.
Some-bod-y laid the moun-tains low_
They watched the ha - zy sun_
B
E
E sus4
Amaj7
A6
while the town got_ high.
sink-ing in the_ sea.
f
E
Esus4
1. Amaj7
A6
E/B
B7
A/E
L.H.
R.H.
decresc.
E
2. Amaj7
A6
G
G sus4
Cmaj7
C6
mp
G
G sus4
Cmaj7
C6
G/D
D7
C/D
rit. e dim.

G6
C sus2
G6
C sus2
G6
C sus2
G6
C sus2
L.H.
a tempo
pp gradual cresc.
G
C
D
G
You can leave it all__ be-hind____ and sail to La-hai - na,____
Who will pro-vide the grand_ de-sign?____ What is yours and what __ is_ mine?
And you can see_ them there____ on Sun-day morn - ing.___
mp-mf-f
C
D
G
just like the mis-sion-ar-ies did__ so man-y years a - go.______
'Cause there is no more new fron - tier;_ we have got to make it here.
Stand up and sing a - bout_ what it's like up there.___
C
D
G
They e-ven brought a ne - on sign:_____ "Je - sus is com - ing."____
We sat-is - fy our end - less needs_____ and jus-ti-fy our blood - y__ deeds
They call it par - a - dise._____ I don't know why.___________

C
1. D
G
Brought the white man's bur - den down,
in the name of des - tin - y
You call some-place par - a - dise,
brought the white man's reign.
2. D
G
G sus4
3. D
and in the name of God.
kiss it good-
G
G sus4
Cmaj7
C6
G
G sus4
bye.
Repeat and fade
Cmaj7
C6
G
G sus4
Cmaj7
C6
Repeat and fade

NEW KID IN TOWN

Words and Music by
JOHN DAVID SOUTHER
DON HENLEY and GLENN FREY

F♯m7 B A B
Great ex - pec - ta - tions, ev-'ry-bod-y's
Hope-less ro - man - tics, here we
E
watch-ing you.
go a - gain.
Peo-ple you meet,
But af-ter a while
F♯m7 B F♯m7 B A
they all seem to know you.
you're look-ing the oth - er way.
It's those
E-ven your old
rest - less
B E G♯sus 4 G♯
4 fr.
friends treat you like you're some-thing new.
hearts that nev - er mend.

C#m
4 fr.
F#
C#m
4 fr.
F#
John-ny-come-late - ly,
John-ny-come-late - ly,
the new kid in town.
the new kid in town.
C#m
4 fr.
F#
1.
F#m7
B
Ev-'ry-bod-y loves — you,
Will she still love — you
so don't — let them down. —
2. F#m7
B
E
A
G#m
4fr.
F#m
E
when you're not a - round? —
B
E
There's so man-y things you should have told — her,

B
C♯m
4 fr.
F♯
but night af-ter night you're will-ing to hold her, just hold her.
Am7
C/D
D7
G
Tears on your shoul-der. There's talk on the street; it's there to re-
Am7
D
Am7
D
C
D
mind you that it does-n't real-ly mat-ter which side
G
you're on. You're walk-ing a-way and they're talk-ing be-

Am7
D
Am7
D
C
hind you. They will nev - er for - get you till
D
G
B7
No chord
some-bod - y new comes a - long.
Em7
A
N.C.
Em7
A
N.C.
Where you been late - ly? There's a new kid in town.
Em7
A
Am7
Ev - 'ry - bod - y loves him, don't they? Now he's hold - ing

B
E
G♯m7
4 fr.
A
3
her, and you're still a - round. Oh, my, my.
There's a new kid in town,
just an-oth-er new kid in town.
Am
Ooh, hoo. Ev-'ry-bod-y's talk-ing 'bout the new kid in town.
C♯m

E
C♯m
4 fr.
Ooh, hoo. Ev - 'ry - bod - y's walk - ing like the
new kid in town. There's a new kid in town.
I don't want to hear it. There's a new kid in town. I don't want to hear it. There's a
Repeat and fade
new kid in town. There's a new kid in town. There's a

HEARTACHE TONIGHT

Words and Music by
DON HENLEY, GLENN FREY,
BOB SEGER and JOHN DAVID SOUTHER

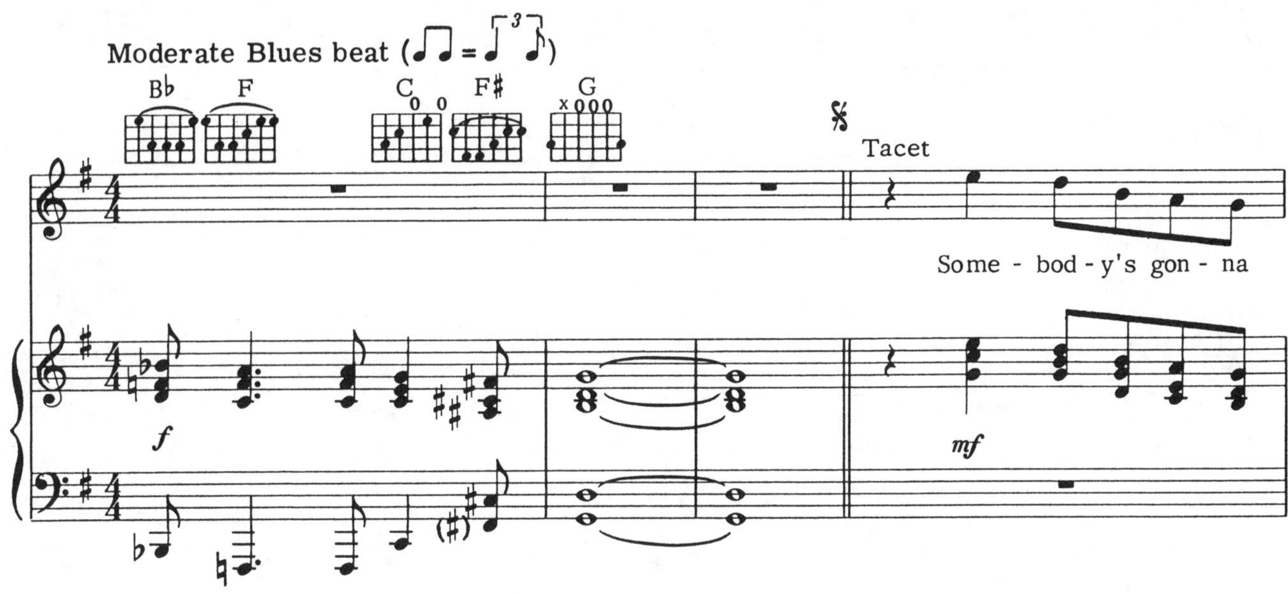

G(no3rd)
3fr.
Em(no3rd)
G(no3rd)
3fr.
Em(no3rd)
Ev-'ry-bod-y wants to touch some - bod - y, if it takes all night.
G(no3rd)
3fr.
C(no3rd)
3fr.
G(no3rd)
3fr.
D(no3rd)
5fr.
Ev-'ry-bod-y wants to take a lit-tle chance, make it come out right.
C7
There's gon-na be a heart - ache to-night, a heart - ache to-night, I know.
G7
C7
There's gon - na be a heart - ache to-night, a

To Coda
A
D
heart - ache to-night, I know.
Lord, I know.
G
Em
G
Some peo-ple like to stay out late.
Some folks can't hold out that
Em
G
C
long.
But no - bod - y wants to go home now;
G
D(no3rd)
5fr.
there's too much go - in' on.

G
Em
G
This night is gon - na last for - ev - er. Last all, last all sum-mer
Em
G
C
long. Some time be-fore the sun comes up
G
D
the ra-di - o is gon - na play that song. There's gon-na be a
C7
G7
heart - ache to-night, a heart - ache to-night, I know.

C7
There's gon-na be a heart - ache to-night, a heart - ache to-night, I know.
A
D
G
Lord, I know. There's gon-na be a heart - ache to-night, the
C
C#o
moon's shin-in' bright, so turn out the light, and we'll get it right. There's gon-na be a
G
D
G
heart- ache to-night, a heart-ache to-night, I know.

Bb F C F# G Bb F C F# G
D. S. 𝄋 al Coda
Coda
A D G
Let's go. We can beat a-round the bush-es; we can
C C#o
get down to the bone; we can leave it in the park-in' lot, but ei-ther way, there's gon-na be a
G D G
heart-ache to-night, a heart - ache to-night, I know. Oh, I

C7
G
D
know. There'll be a heart - ache to-night, a heart-ache to-night, I know.
G
B♭
F
C
F♯
G
B♭
F
C
F♯
G
B♭
F
C
F♯
G
B♭
F
C
G

PLEASE COME HOME FOR CHRISTMAS

Words and Music by
CHARLES BROWN
and GENE REDD

A
D
A
F♯m7
gone,_ I have no friends_ to wish me
B7
E
E+
greet - ings__ once a - gain. Choirs___ will be
A
Amaj7
A7
sing - ing "Si - lent Night,"___ Christ - mas
D
B7/D♯
car - ols by___ can - dle - light. Please_ come home for

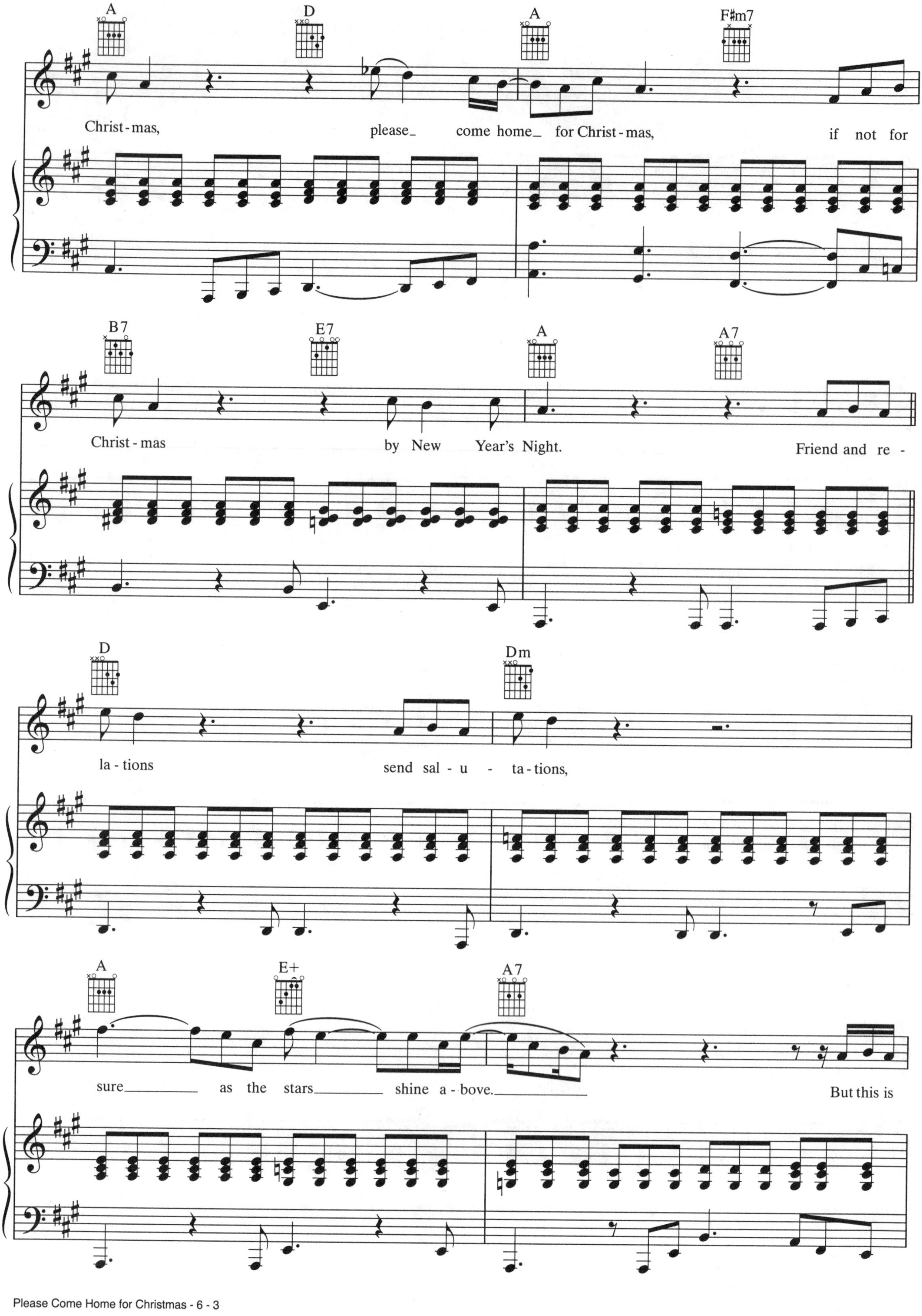

A D A F♯m7

Christ - mas, please_ come home_ for Christ - mas, if not for

B7 E7 A A7

Christ - mas by New Year's Night. Friend and re -

D Dm

la - tions send sal - u - ta - tions,

D
Dm
Christ-mas, yes,___ Christ-mas, my dear,_ the time of
B7
E
E+
year___ to be_ with the one you love._ So won't you
A
Amaj7
A7
tell me you'll_ nev-er more roam._ Christ-mas and
D
B7/D♯
New Year will_ find you home. There'll be no more

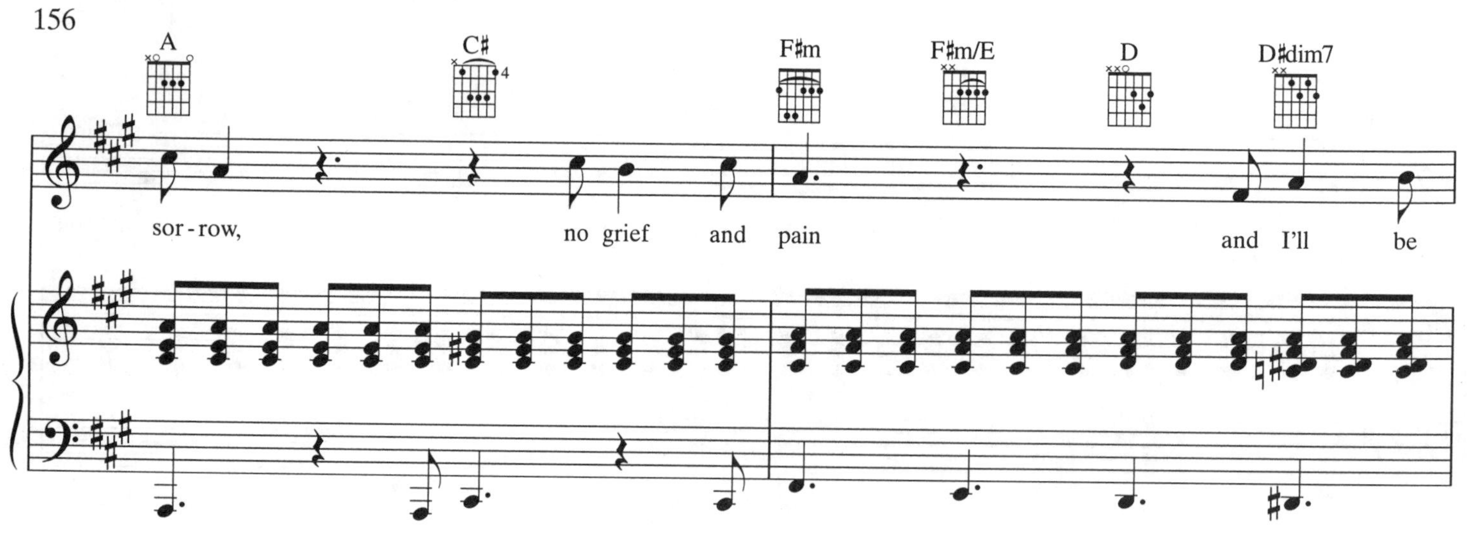
A
C♯
F♯m
F♯m/E
D
D♯dim7
sor - row, no grief and pain and I'll be

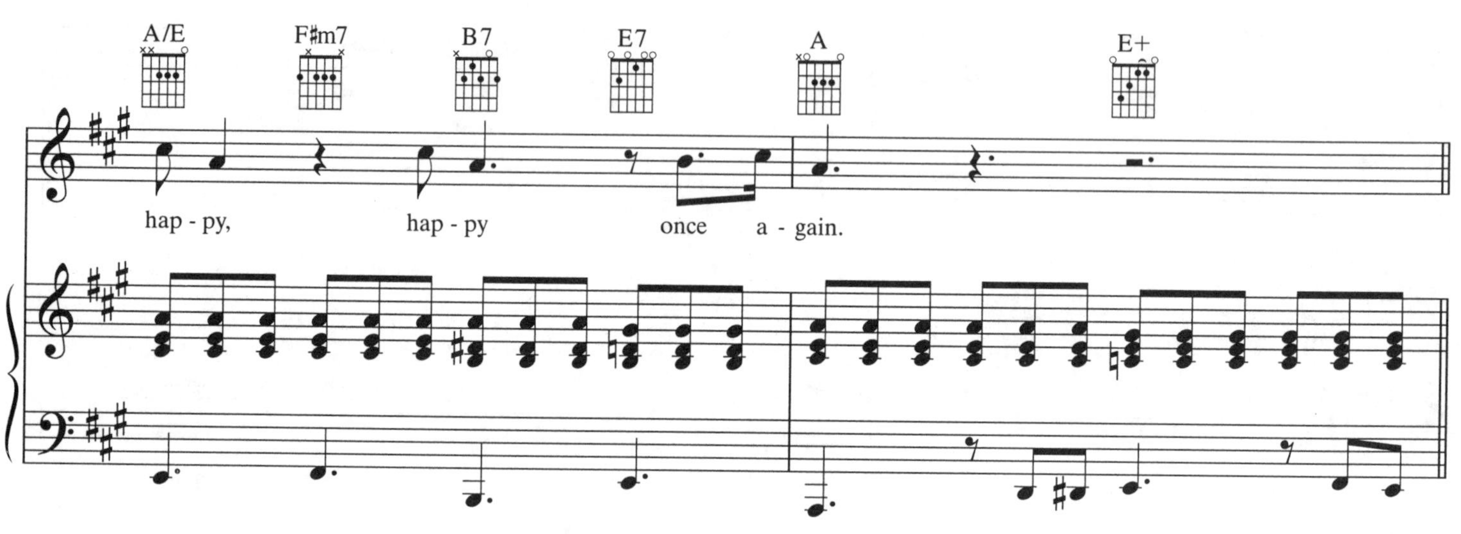
A/E
F♯m7
B7
E7
A
E+
hap - py, hap - py once a - gain.

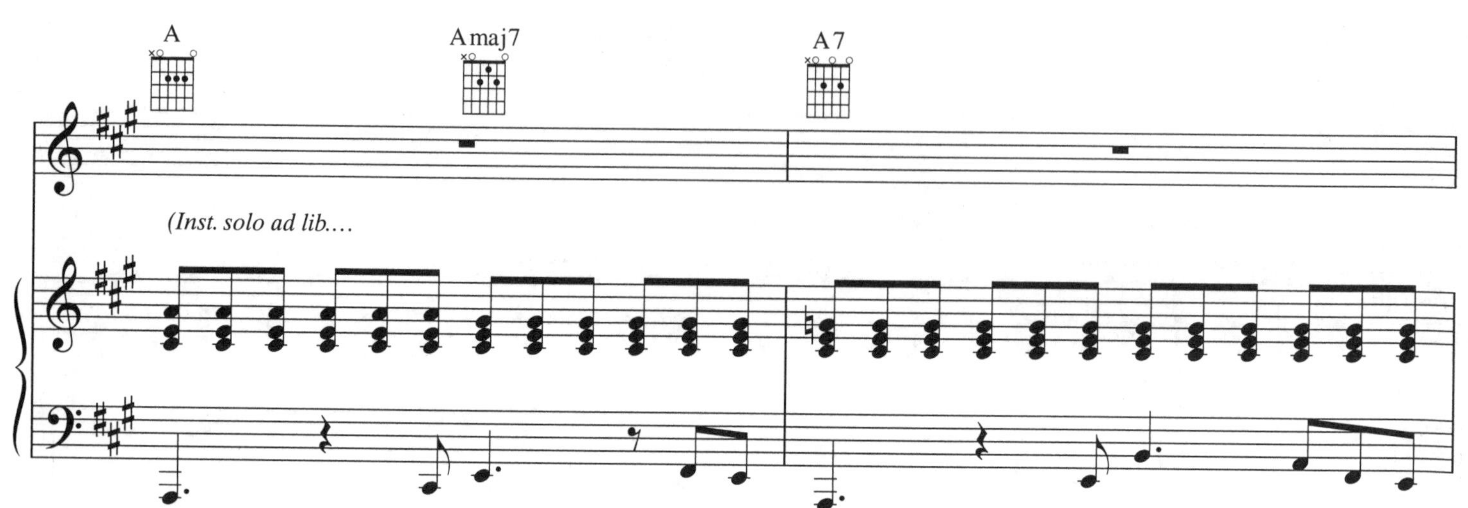
A
A maj7
A7
(Inst. solo ad lib....

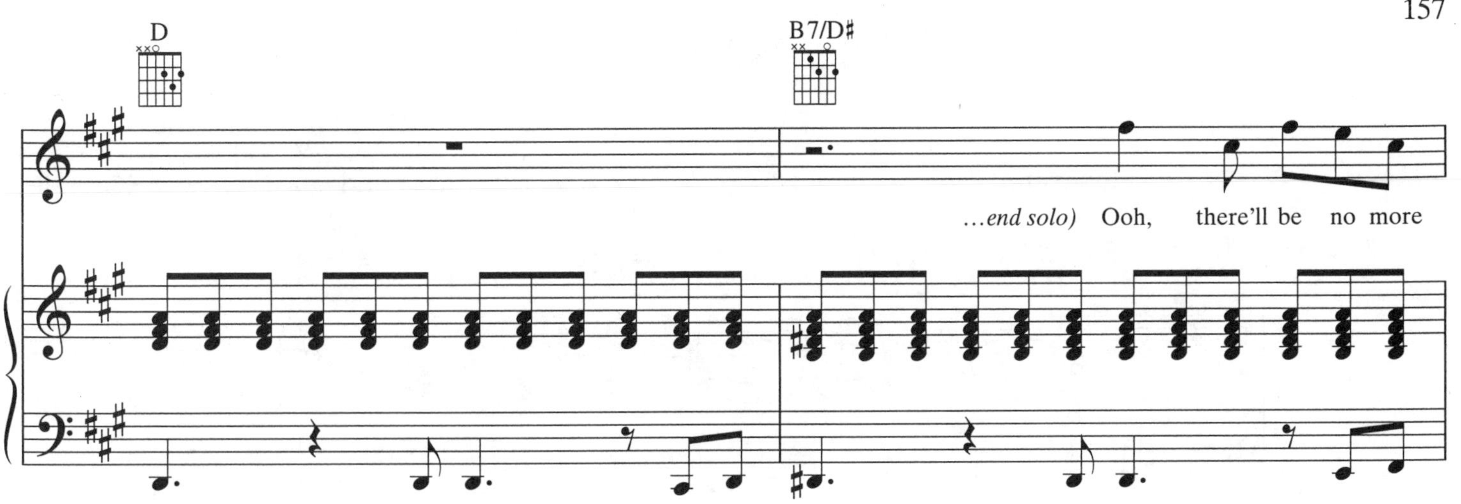
D
B7/D♯
…end solo) Ooh, there'll be no more

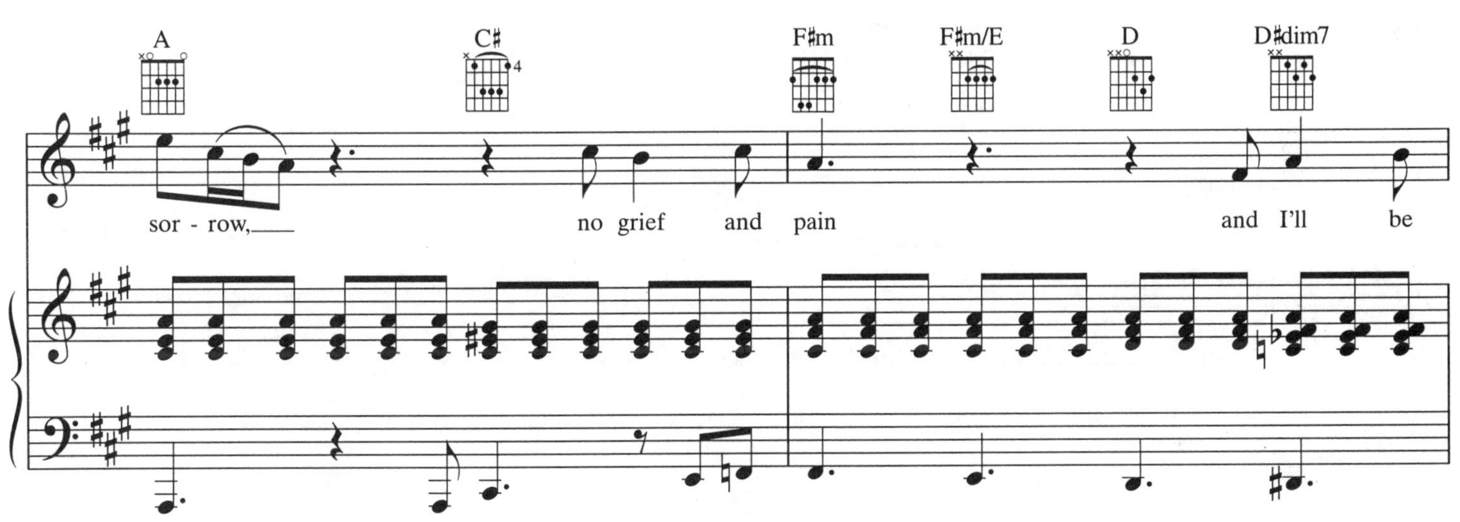
A
C♯
F♯m
F♯m/E
D
D♯dim7
sor - row, no grief and pain and I'll be

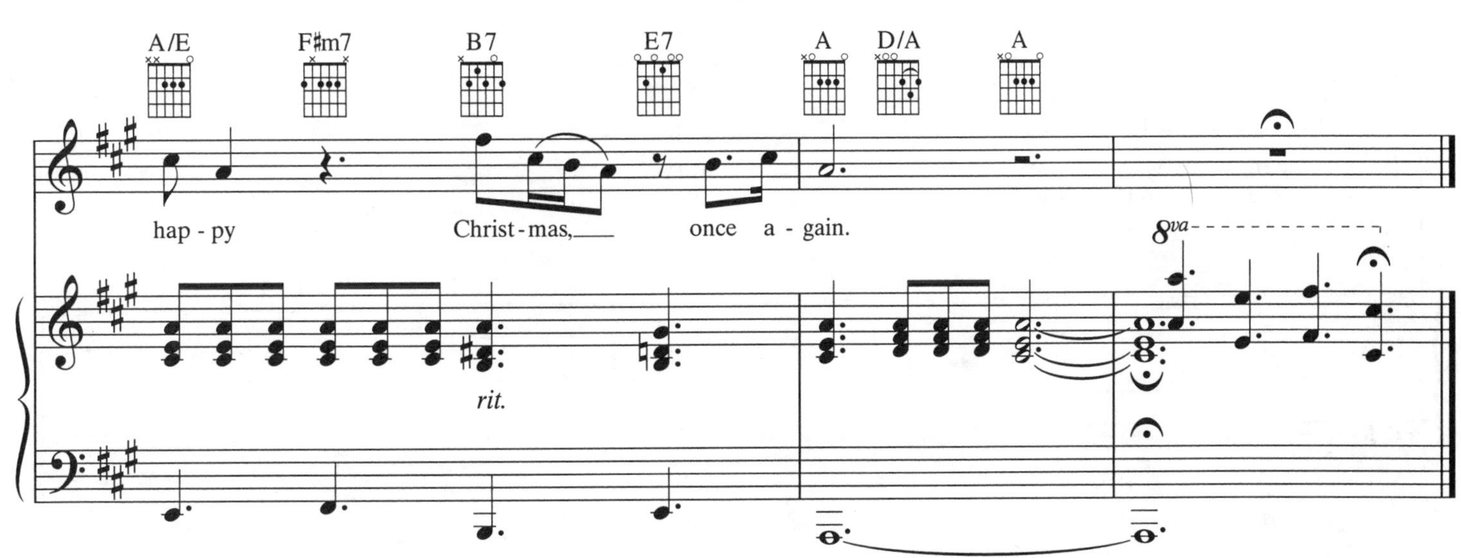
A/E
F♯m7
B7
E7
A
D/A
A
hap - py Christ - mas, once a - gain.
rit.
8va

THE SAD CAFÉ

Words and Music by
DON HENLEY, GLENN FREY,
JOE WALSH and JOHN DAVID SOUTHER

Em
F#7sus4
The tracks that ran down the boul - e - vard had
And we would sing right out loud the
But things in this life change ver - y slow - ly, if they
F#7
B
Em
all been washed a - way.
things we could not say.
ev - er change at all.
Out of the sil -
We thought we could change
There's no use in ask -
F#7(add B)
B
ver light, the past came soft - ly call -
this world with words like "love" and "free -
ing why; it just turned out that way.

Em
F#7sus4
ing. And I re-mem-ber the times we spent in-
dom." We were part of the lone - ly crowd in-
So meet me at mid - night, babe, in-
To Coda
F#7
B
1.
2.
side the Sad Ca-fé.
side the Sad Ca-fé.
side the Sad Ca-fé.
G#m
4 fr.
D#m
6 fr.
Oh, ex-pect-ing to fly, we would
G#m
4 fr.
C#m7
4 fr.
F#6
F#
meet on that beau-ti-ful shore in the sweet by-and - by.

B
Em
F#7(add B)
Some of their dreams came true,
B
some just passed a - way.
C#m7-5
F#7sus4
And some of them stayed be - hind in -
F#7
B
side the Sad Ca - fé.
The

F♯7sus4
F♯7
F♯7sus4
F♯7
clouds rolled in and hid that shore.
E/F♯
G♯m/F♯
F♯
E/F♯
F♯7sus4
F♯7
Now that Glo - ry Train, it don't stop here no more.
Bm7/E
E7
Now I look at the years gone by, and
Bm7/E
E7
won - der at the pow - ers that be.

C♯m7/F♯
F♯7
I don't know why for - tune smiles on some,
C♯m7/F♯
F♯7
D. S. 𝄋 al Coda 𝄌
F♯
Coda
and lets the rest go free.
C♯m7-5
F♯7sus4
F♯7
B
Why don't you meet me at mid - night, babe, in - side the Sad Ca - fé.
Repeat and fade
B
C♯m7-5
F♯7sus4
F♯7
B
Repeat and fade

I CAN'T TELL YOU WHY

A/B
Gmaj7
F#7sus4
F#7
walk a- way, some-thin' makes me turn a - round and stay, and I
Bm
To Coda
A/B
G
F#m7
can't tell you why.
Dmaj7
Gmaj7
When we get cra - zy, it just ain't right. Girl, I get lone - ly, too.
(Try to keep your head, lit- tle girl.)
Dmaj7
You don't have to wor -ry. Just hold on tight,
(Don't get caught in your

Gmaj7
F#7sus4
F#7
Bm
'cause I love you.
little world.
Oh.)
Noth-in's wrong as far as
A/B
Gmaj7
F#7sus4
F#7
I can see.
We make it hard-er than it has to be, and I
Bm
A/B
Gmaj7
can't tell you why.
No, ba-by, I can't tell you why.
F#7sus4
F#7
Gmaj7
F#m7
I can't tell you why.

Bm7
A/B
N.C.
Bm7
F♯m7
N.C.
R.H.
L.H.
D.S.𝄋 al Coda 𝄌
Coda
A/B
Gmaj7
No, no, ba-by, I can't tell_ you why._
R.H.
F♯7sus4
F♯7
Gmaj7
F♯m7
I ___ can't tell_ you why.___
Repeat and fade
Gmaj7
F♯m7
Gmaj7
F♯m7
I can't tell_you why.___
Repeat and fade

THE LONG RUN

Words and Music by
DON HENLEY and GLEN FREY

F
C
stay out till the break of day.
the cra - zy things that you do.
Oh, that did-n't git it; it was
'Cause all the deb - u - tantes in
F
high time I quit it. I just could - n't car - ry on that way.
Hous - ton, ba - by, could - n't hold a can - dle to you.
Am
Oh, I did some dam-age, I know it's true. Did-n't
Did you do it for love? Did you do it for mon-ey? Did you
F
know I was so lone - ly till I found you.
do it for spite? Did you think you had to, hon - ey?

C
You can go the dis - tance. We'll find out in the
Who is gon - na make it? We'll find out in the
F
C
long run (in the long run). We can han - dle some re-sis-tance
long run (in the long run). I know we can take it
F
if our love is a strong one (is a strong one). Peo - ple
if our love is a strong one (is a strong one). Well, we're
Am
F
talk-in' a -bout us; they got noth - in' else to do. When it all comes down we will
scared, but we ain't shak - in'. Kind-a bent, but we ain't

C
F
still come through in the long run. Ooh, I want to tell you, it's a
break-in'. In the long run. Ooh, I want to tell you, it's a
1.
C
G
G7
Tacet
2. C
F
long run. You know, I long run. In the
C
F
C
G
long run. In the long run.
Repeat (vocal ad lib) and fade
C
F
Repeat and fade

IN THE CITY

Words and Music by
JOE WALSH and BARRY DeVORZON

E
A
D
E/D
bet - ter, ___
pret - ty. ___
but there's no - where else in
No one's there to catch you when you
A
E
D
A
sight.
fall.
It's sur - viv - al in the
Some - where out ___ on that ho -
E
A
D
A
cit - y ___
ri - zon, ___
when you live ___ from day to day. ___
far a - way ___ from the ne - on sky, ___
E
A
D
A
City streets don't have much
I know there must be some - thin'

E
A
D
E/D
pit - y.
bet - ter,
When you're down, that's where you'll
and I can't stay an - oth - er
cresc.
A
Bm7/A
E/A
stay:
night
in the cit - y, oh,
in the cit - y, oh,
f
D/A
Bm/A
To Coda
A
Bm7/A
oh.
oh.
In the
E/A
Bm7/A
A
G
cit - y.

D
A
E
A
D
A
D. S. 𝄋 al Coda ⊕
E
A
D
A
E
A
Coda
Repeat and fade
A
Bm7/A
In the
Repeat and fade
E/A
Bm7/A
cit - y.

THOSE SHOES

Words and Music by
DON HENLEY, GLENN FREY
and DON FELDER

Em7
In the mid-dle of the tall drinks and the dra - ma,
You got to have your in - de - pend - ence,
Em
there must be some-one you know.
but you don't know just where to start.
G(no3rd)
3fr.
God knows, you're look-ing good e-nough, but you're so smooth and the world's
Des-per - a - tion in the sing-les bars an' all those jerk-offs in their
You just want some-one to talk to. They just wan - na get their
A(no3rd)
so rough.
fan - cy cars;
hands on you.
You might have some-thin' to lose.
you can't be - lieve your re - views.
You get what - ev - er you choose.

C(no3rd)
3fr.
B(no3rd)
Oh, no, pret - ty ma - ma, what you gon - na
Oh, no, you can't do that, once you've start - ed
Oh, no, you can't do that, once you've start - ed
Em
do in those shoes?
wear - in' those shoes.
wear - in' those shoes.
To Coda
1.
2.
N.C.
They're look - in' at you, lean - in' on you,
tell you an - y - thing you wan - na hear.
They give you

tab - lets of love.
They're wait - ing for you,
got to score you,
hand - y with the shov - el and so sin - cere.
Ooh,
they got the kid glove.
D. S. 𝄋 al Coda
Coda

SEVEN BRIDGES ROAD

Words and Music by
STEVE YOUNG

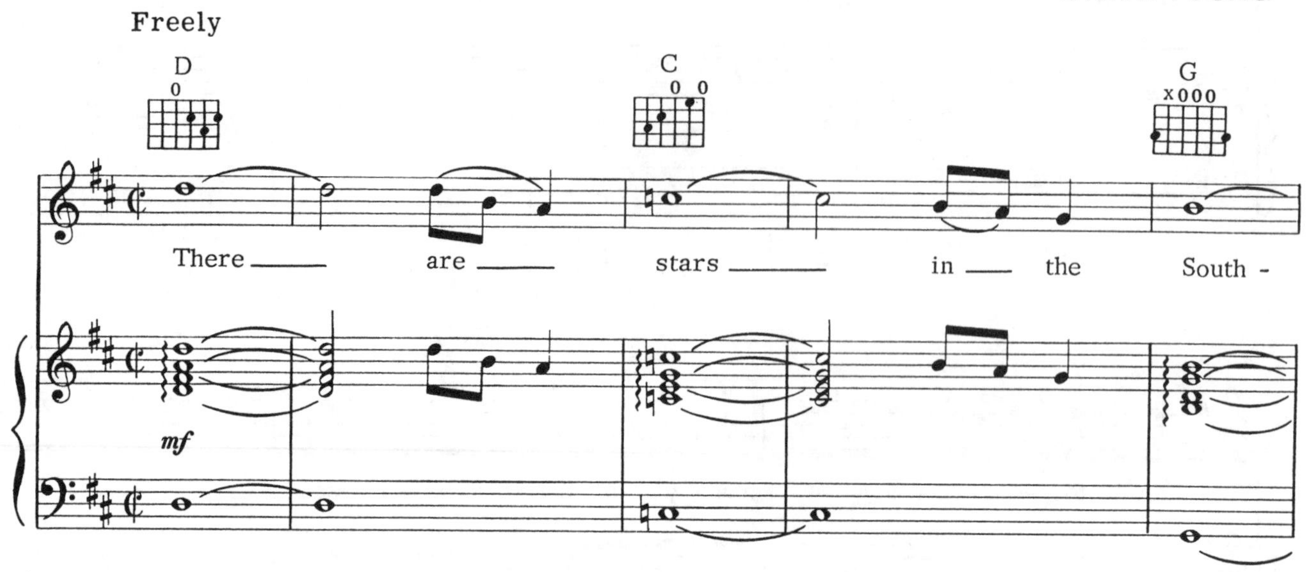

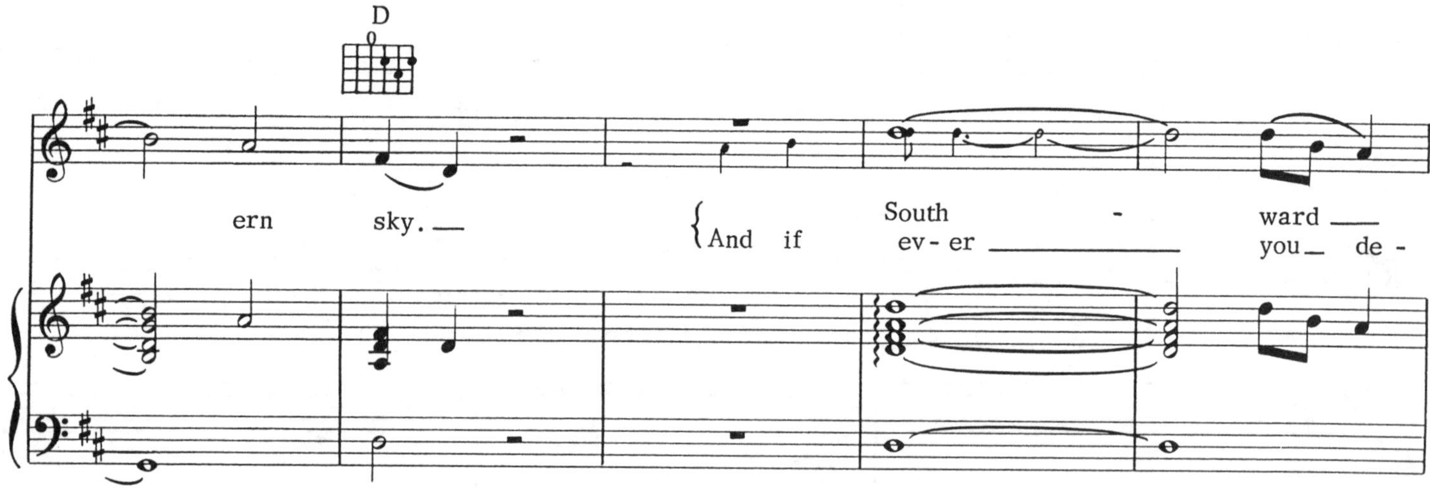

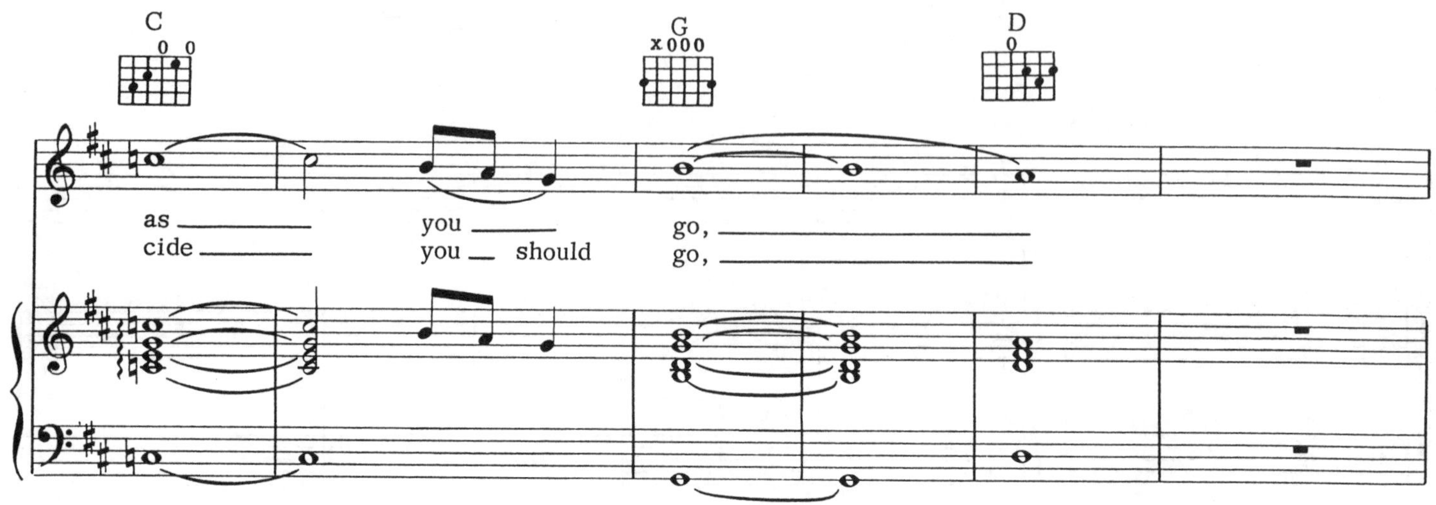

C
G
there is moon - light and moss
there is a taste of time -
D
in the trees
sweet - ened hon - ey
down the Sev - en
C
To Coda
G
Bright Country beat
D
Bridg - es Road.

D
C
Now, I have loved
I have loved
G
D
you like a ba - by,
you in a tame way and
C
G
like some lone - some child.
I have loved you wild.
D
1.
And

2.
C
Some - times
D
there's a part of me
C
has to turn from here and
D
go,

C
run - ning
like
a child
from
D
these
warm
stars
down the
Sev -
C
G
en
Bridg
-
es
Road.
D
D. C. al Coda
Coda
G
D
Road.

LOVE WILL KEEP US ALIVE

D2(6)
You were search - ing ___ for a place to hide. ___
The world is chang - ing ___ right be - fore your eyes. ___
When we're hun - gry ___ love will keep us a -
Esus
E
A2
live. ___
Lost and lone - ly, ___
Now I've found ___ you, ___
(Instrumental solo . . .
F♯m11
now you've giv - en me ___ the will ___ to sur - vive. ___
there's no more ___ emp - ti - ness ___ in - side. ___
When we're
When we're

To Coda
1.
D2(6)
Esus
E
A2
hun - gry, love will keep us a - live.
hun - gry, love will keep us a - live.
2.3.
A2
2. Don't you
. . . end solo)
I would
Bridge:
D
F♯m7
die for you,
climb the high - est moun -

Bm7
- tain.
Ba - by,
there's noth-ing I
would-n't
E
E/D
1.
D.S. 𝄋
C♯m7
E/B
2.
D.S. 𝄋 al Coda
C♯m7
E/B
do.
3. Now, I've
4. I was
Coda
A2
F♯m11
When
we're

D2(6)
Esus
E
A2
hun - gry, love will keep us a - live.
F♯m11
D2(6)
Esus
When we're hun - gry, love will keep us a - live.
A2
rit.

GET OVER IT

Words and Music by
DON HENLEY and GLENN FREY

Verse:
D5
turn on the tube, what do I see? A whole lot of peo-ple cry-in',
2.3. (See additional lyrics)
"Don't blame me." They point their crook-ed lit-tle fin-gers at ev-'ry-bod-y else,
G
spend all their time feel-ing sor-ry for them-selves. Vic-tim of this,
A
vic-tim of that. Your ma-ma's too thin and your dad-dy's too fat. 1. Get ov-

Chorus:
D5
F
- er it.
2.3. (See additional lyrics)
Get ov - er it.
G
All this whin-in', and cry - in', and pitch-in' a fit. Get ov -
D5
To Coda
- er it, get ov - er it.
(Guitar solo ad. lib . . .
F

G
D5
1.
2.
Bridge:
C
. . . end solo) 2. You say you . . . end solo) It's like go-ing to con-fes-sion ev-'ry-time I hear you speak.
D5
C
You're mak-in' the most of your los - ing streak.
A
D.S. 𝄋 al Coda
Some call it sick and I call it weak.
Yeah, yeah, yeah, yeah. 3. You

Coda
- er it, get ov - er it. Get ov -
F
- er it. It's got - ta stop some-time, so
G
why don't you quit? Get ov - er it. Get ov - er it.
D5
tacet
D5
F

Verse 2:
You say you haven't been the same since you had your little crash
But you might feel better if they gave you some cash.
The more I think about it, old Billy was right.
Let's kill all the lawyers, kill 'em tonight.
You don't want to work, you want to live like a king
But the big bad world doesn't owe you a thing.
(To Chorus:)

Chorus 2:
Get over it,
Get over it.
If you don't want to play, then you might as well split.
Get over it, get over it.

Verse 3:
You drag it around like a ball and chain,
You wallow in the guilt, you wallow in the pain.
You wave it like a flag, you wear it like a crown,
Got your mind in the gutter bringin' everybody down.
You bitch about the present, you blame it on the past.
I'd like to find your inner child and kick it's little ass.
(To Chorus:)

Chorus 3:
Get over it.
Get over it.
All this bitchin', and moanin', and pitchin' a fit.
Get over it, get over it.

HOLE IN THE WORLD

Words and Music by
DON HENLEY and GLENN FREY

Verse:

A F♯m7 E

1. They say that an - ger is just love dis - a - point - ed.
2. Oh they tell me there's a place o - ver yon - der.

(Oo, oo, oo.

A F♯m7 E

They say that love is just a state of mind.
Cool wa - ter run - ning through the burn - ing sand.

Oo, oo, oo.

A F♯m7 E C♯m

But all this fight - ing o - ver who is an - noint - ed,
Un - til we learn to love one an - oth - er,

Oo, oo, oo.

F♯m E A

oh, how can peo - ple be so blind.
we will nev - er reach the prom - ised land.

Oo, oo, oo.)

There's a

Chorus:
F♯m7
E
D
hole
in
the
world
to
-
night.
There's
a
A
F♯m7
E
D
cloud
of
fear
and
sor
-
row.
There's
a
A
F♯m7
E
C♯m
hole
in
the
world
to
-
night.
Don't
let
there
be
a
F♯m
E
A
1.
2.
hole
in
the world
to
-
mor
-
row.
row.
There's
a

B
G♯m
F♯
E
They say that an - ger is just love dis - ap - point - ed.
hole in the world to - night. There's a
B
G♯m
F♯
E
B
G♯m
F♯
They say that love is just a state of mind.
But all this fight-ing o - ver
cloud of fear and sor - row. There's a hole in the world to - night.
D♯m
G♯m
F♯
B
who will be an - noint - ed,
oh, how can peo - ple be so blind.
Don't let there be a hole in the world to - mor - row. There's a

a capella
N.C.
hole in the world to - night. There's a
cloud of fear and sor - row. There's a
hole in the world to - night. Don't let there be a
hole in the world to - mor - row. There's a

B
G♯m7
F♯
E
hole in the world to - night.
There's a
cloud of fear and sor - row.
There's a
D♯m
Don't let there be a
G♯m
hole in the world to - mor - row.
Repeat ad lib. and fade

EAGLES

DESPERADO

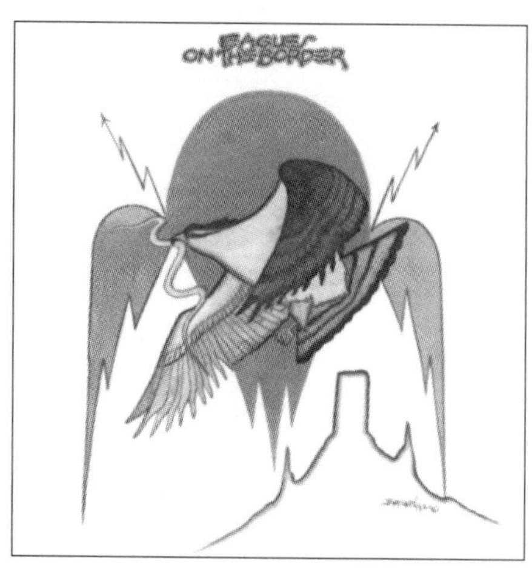

ON THE BORDER

ONE OF THESE NIGHTS

THEIR GREATEST HITS, 1971—1975

HOTEL CALIFORNIA

THE LONG RUN

EAGLES LIVE

**GREATEST HITS,
VOLUME 2**

HELL FREEZES OVER

**SELECTED WORKS
1972–1999**

Photo: James R. Minch